Confidence When It Counts:

Rise Above Self-Criticism and Bias to Make Your Mark

By Sharon Melnick, PhD

For information and request for permission, please contact me:

Email: **Sharon@SharonMelnick.com**

FREE RESOURCES

Download key exercises from this book and receive a free video training to speak up with confidence even if you don't have all the answers. Simply visit **http://www.doubtfreenow.com**.

Want to share your thoughts and learn from other readers of the book? Get updates and Join the movement at www.facebook.com/groups/confidencecounts/.

Want my help to have Confidence when it Counts or want to bring these tools via training to your colleagues (or your daughter/son/niece/mentee)? Want the confidence to get promoted, expand your role and have greater influence in your organization and community?   Discover how at **http://www.sharonmelnick.com**

NAFE Twin Cities Women's Leadership Summit

June 8, 2017

U.S. Bank is proud to sponsor the National Association for Female Executives (NAFE) Twin Cities Women's Leadership Summit.

This year's book, "Confidence When it Counts: Rise Above Self-Criticism and Bias to Make Your Mark" by keynote speaker Sharon Melnick, is the inspiration for today's event. It focuses on elevating women's confidence within their organizations and helping them achieve their career goals. U.S. Bank is thrilled to give each of you a copy of the book.

We're also excited to come together with other female business leaders for this event. We are so fortunate to have an amazing community of professional women in our region, and it's our opportunity and responsibility to support them.

At U.S. Bank, more than 60 percent of our workforce is comprised of women, which is best in class. We're proud to have women serve on our Managing Committee and Board of Directors. We're also committed to advancing and retaining women through our U.S. Bank Women Business Resource Group. U.S. Bank Women provides employees with opportunities to network, learn, develop leadership skills and contribute to business results.

While we're proud of our efforts to support women, we know there's still work to do. As business leaders, we owe it to our female employees to close the pay gap, provide advancement opportunities and support them throughout their careers.

Events like this one help us start the conversation and generate new ideas. We look forward to today's discussion.

Sincerely,

Jennie Carlson
Executive Vice President, Human Resources, U.S. Bank

Table of Contents

Introduction

There you are, just going through your day. You feel good about how you've been able to add value and make a difference for others. Yes, you have too much to do and there are far too many expectations of you. And no, you're not as far along as you might want to be in your career and you hope that breakthrough will, somehow, come soon. But, despite the obstacles, you enjoy your work, the people, and your outside-of-work life.

Then . . . BOOM!

Out of the blue, a situation happens that hijacks you. Your feelings about yourself rush to the fore, and the response you show will determine how your life moves forward from that point on.

What are these moments when confidence counts? Well, there are the *public* moments:

- When interacting with someone's strong personality . . . do you take it personally and react, or do you stay poised and forgive their limitations?
- When a senior leader fires a question or pushes back on your idea . . . do you freeze, or speak up and respectfully stand your ground?
- When you're preparing to speak in front of a large room . . . do you enjoy the opportunity to educate or are you full of nerves and dread?
- When stating your fee . . . do you own your value and stick to your number, or do you not feel worth it and want to keep expectations low?
- When networking . . . do you compare yourself and hesitate, or do you enjoy being yourself?

And then there are *private* moments where confidence counts:

- When you've just finished a presentation . . . do you critique your flaws or feel satisfied at the value you brought?
- When considering your next chapter . . . do you say, "I'm not ready" or do you trust you'll make it work?
- When fielding demands from your family . . . do you feel deserving of self-care or stretch yourself too thin for others?
- When you don't hear back from a new person you're dating do you have perspective or feel unworthy?
- When you have that gnawing frustration you're not where you want to be in your career . . . do you beat yourself up? Resent the difficult person and the politics that thwarted you? Or rise above bias and influence the situation toward your desired outcome?

These, and many others, are the moments when confidence counts. How you show up in these moments will determine . . . well, everything.

At least it did for me.

In August of 2000, I had tickets to a rock concert in Washington, D.C. One of those blockbuster lineups with all your favorite musicians. At the time, I lived in Cambridge, Massachusetts, so needed to fly in order to get to the concert. I arrived as the stands were just starting to fill and happened to notice a small cluster of people standing over to my left. As I looked a little closer, I was stunned to realize that I recognized one woman in the group.

It was Tipper Gore, wife of then sitting vice president, Al Gore.

On instinct, and without over-thinking it, I marched right over to her. I reached out my hand towards her and confidently said, "Hi! I'm Dr. Sharon Melnick. I do psychology research at Harvard Medical School. My research is on how women can have resilience and confidence, even when they've grown up in difficult circumstances. I thought you might be interested in that, since you're a champion for women's empowerment."

Tipper's interest was piqued, so we began talking about her different initiatives. As the conversation unfolded, she shared with me that her daughter, Sara – "who's at Harvard" – was going through her own challenges and wins. We commiserated, and I offered to connect her with some of my Harvard resources.

Essentially, we had one of those 'girlfriend' moments.

At that point, Tipper turned to her Chief of Staff and said, "Melissa, could you get Dr. Melnick's contact information? We want to invite her to the White House to share the policy implications of her research."

On the flight back home, I began thinking how lucky I am that I've always known – since age 5 – what work I wanted to do in the world.

Improving the lives of millions of women and their families was the reason why I sacrificed my way through 11 years of education and took joy in poring over academic research. My entire life had been dedicated to giving each woman an opportunity to make the contribution she was put here to make.

THIS was my dream.

Once home, I put some effort into writing a short description of the research I was spearheading at Harvard. At that time, early in my career, we were mapping the intergenerational cycle to understand what a person carries forward into adulthood from experiences in childhood. Building on the brilliant research of my mentor, Dr. Karlen Lyons-Ruth, I developed new methods for women and men from difficult childhoods to avoid repeating mistakes of their parents. These methods showed promising results by quickly helping them 'get out of their own way' and live up to their potential – in career and in life.

A few weeks later, I was lacing up my sneakers to go for a run on a balmy Monday evening. The phone rings, showing a caller ID with "202" area code, along with some indecipherable codes that included "Gov." I'm shocked and brace myself to pick up the phone.

"Hi Sharon, it's Melissa. From Tipper Gore's office."

We chat, and she outlines Tipper's initiatives to help women around the country, including various program offerings, publicity campaigns, and policy maker gatherings. I'm noting that the reach of their interventions is vast. My heart was racing with nervous excitement.

Then Melissa 'pops the question': "We'd like to know if you will come down to the White House to share the policy implications of your research?"

What an honor! I have a vivid image of myself sitting around the table at the White House, presenting this groundbreaking research to other thought leaders, policy makers, and even celebrities.

Naturally, what do you think my response was?

Of course. I said, "No."

Well, I didn't exactly say "no," but I did put off the invitation.

"I'm not sure we know enough yet from the research. Let me get back to you when we know a little more."

But the implication was there. I'd said 'no' to an invitation from the White House. (That's fine, go ahead and gasp.)

You see, even though I had been told repeatedly that I was really good at my job, I didn't feel it 'in my bones.' I thought that if I showed up at the White House, I'd be found out – an imposter who was 'not smart enough.'

Even though I could have offered insights to that esteemed group that no one else in the world would have been able to provide, I honestly thought, "I'm not good enough, I'm not ready."

Even though it would have sounded cool to say I had presented to changemakers at the White House, I didn't feel worthy of a seat at that table.

Besides, I was already overwhelmed with my *busy* life. I didn't think I could handle any more.

At least, that's what I told myself in that moment that determined the course for my professional life.

So, in the moment when it counted, **I listened to my critical, doubting inner voice. I made a decision that prioritized my own self-evaluation over the contribution I could have made to millions of people.**

Have you ever had a White House moment where you didn't feel ready for, or worthy of saying yes to an important step in your career and life?

Are you experiencing the success and the ease that you truly want – or are you only living the life you think you deserve, one that you've settled for after years of frustration.

Is there a next level dream you've yet to start?

Are you talented and smart, but underutilized and under-recognized…seeking a way to be a bigger version of yourself so you can get to the next level?

As a woman who is ready to expand your income, your influence, and your impact, what if I told you it was possible, in every moment that counts, to have the confidence to fulfill your potential and make a difference – and that you could gain that confidence *in moments or days*? Would you believe me?

That's what you'll get in this book. It's the book I wish I'd had, the one that every woman who wants to have a big impact needs. The one that every woman who has learned these techniques asks me to write for her daughter. It's for you, the woman is highly competent and credentialed but still doubts herself . . . who knows 'in your mind' you are REALLY good at what you do, but you don't feel it "in your bones"...who is self-aware and has come so far but confidence still wavers in the face of difficult people. It's for the woman (namely, most of you, if statistics are right) who's experienced your share of gender bias and then started to question yourself.

What you want is to be able to **end your doubt and start having a deep trust in yourself**. Not just to have confidence when it's easy (like after your boss compliments you, or with clients and family members who love you), but confidence in the heat of the moment when you need it most. When people are difficult or intimidating, you want to stay calm and take the emotionality out of the situation. You want freedom from your harsh self-criticism and to feel comfortable promoting yourself and selling your services. You want to come across as confident, not arrogant or strident, owning your value from within rather than being held back by your perceived weaknesses. You want to have a comfortable sense of where to set your boundaries. You want to influence others to move past their bias, greenlight your advancement and funding, and detach from the frustrations that have worn you down.

You want to effortlessly say YES to opportunities and create even more impactful opportunities for others. You want to earn a higher income and share it by giving back to your family and community. You want to do all this without the stress and harsh or fearful self talk that pops up to shroud your potential for success. In essence, you want the answer to – how can you be successful by being authentically you?

This book will show you how you can become that confident contributor within minutes and days.

This book will give you a toolkit to rise above moments of doubt, fear, and self-criticism to show up as the best version of yourself and act with confidence toward your long-term goals. You will be able to rise above the 'small game' of your personal concerns and play a 'bigger game' in which you can contribute for the good of all involved. You will free up some of the time, energy and attention drained away by self-criticism and self-doubt and put them towards your personal advancement and if you choose, toward advocating for organizational and societal advances in gender parity.

And by consistently acting this way, you can achieve the end result of broad-based influence, abundant income, and a lasting impact on your life.

In short, this book is the instruction manual to 'get out of your own way' and 'get others out of your way'! (And thank you for asking…Yes I did get to present at the White House – in 2015!! And I've used the tools in this book to say "Yes" to over 30 companies in the Fortune 500 and train on hundreds of stages for women around the world…) You too can use these tools to say Yes and make the difference YOU are here for!

If you are a "quick start" and want to get started with the tools, then jump right to Chapter 2. If you want to know more about who this book is for, what you'll get, and why the fast and lasting tools you'll learn will 'stick' even when other tips you've learned haven't, then read on.

This book is for you if:

You work in an organization and want to be a bold leader. You want to or are moving into a new role and you want to be even more influential. You are great at what you do and you want to consistently speak up in meetings with senior leaders. You want to step back from your perfectionistic focus on detail and be a strategic leader. You want to have faith in yourself and be unflappable in the public forums that count. You want productivity with more peace of mind. You want to know how to be confident (not arrogant) and achieve respect anytime you walk into the room. You're frustrated you are not as far along in your career as you'd like to be and you want to advocate for yourself more effectively and move past the decision-maker bias that has overlooked your talents.

If you have been a confident leader in the past and your confidence has been worn down by bias. You'll learn how to get your mojo back and re-energize yourself to take on your forward-looking goals. The tools in this book will support you as you finally achieve the advancement you've been aiming for.

You're an entrepreneur, small business owner, or responsible for developing a business and you are ready to bring in the biggest clients/deals of your career. You're smart and really good at what you do, but don't always feel that about yourself in the moments that count. You want to break away from the pack and shift from chasing after clients to getting chased! You know your success will only come when you 'put yourself out there,' get in front of people, pick up the phone, make appointments – in short, present yourself as confident. You want to become the 'go to' expert in your field. You want to reel in the bigger fish and play a bigger game in your business. You want rapid growth and to still have a business that supports your chosen lifestyle.

It is for you if you are a perfectionist about your work and it's hard to trust other people so you can free yourself up for the next level and to trust yourself to take risks and grow. If your hard work has already led to success and you are frustrated by the lower rate of women receiving funding to take their business to the next level. If you work in a big company, and are irked when you experience that women sometimes get fewer resources and 'at bats' with the big fish clients.

OR

You're just fine in your professional life. It's your personal life where your confidence counts. Speaking up, setting boundaries with your family of origin, with significant others, and in your dating life.

. . . those are the areas in which you could use a change.

I know this 'isn't your first rodeo.' I know you've tried to be more confident and turn down the volume on your self-criticism. You've probably applied the advice of blogs, been inspired by stories of other women at conferences, taken to heart the encouragement of your girlfriends and mentors, maybe even had a coach. Here's why this book is different from other resources you've turned to build your confidence.

1. **Gives you a Toolkit** – This book will give you concrete solutions. Rather than just describing the problem and offering well-meaning but vague encouragements such as 'believe in yourself,' you'll be given specific, proven, and actionable TOOLS to have *confidence across the common situations when it counts*.

This book provides specific advice that will help you re-script those moments that count: How to speak up when facing someone intimidating. How to feel worthy of raising your hand for the next level assignment or asking for a higher fee. How to keep your boundaries when asked to do something you don't want to do. How to not react. How to speak up when fearful what others will think, how to know when you are ready and when you aren't. How to rise above bias, etc.

The solutions you'll find in this book have been proven to help over 19,000 women (and men) around the world, from entry- to mid- to senior-level employees – corporate leaders, business owners, small companies, and nonprofit employees from a variety of ethnicities in 17 countries around the world. These tactics will work for YOU, too.

Although aimed at women, the tools in this book are applicable to men, men and women of color, and any person who finds themselves in a non-majority status where it's important to have confidence.

2. **Customized to your Confidence Type** – Although the term 'confidence' tends to be regarded as a monolith, it's not a one-size-fits-

all concept. It covers a variety of behaviors that fit into 4 'confidence types.' For example, some of you might be perfectionists and judge yourself harshly, but you rarely procrastinate; some of you may hesitate to speak up in a meeting or react defensively but you'd rarely please others.

You might play parts of all of these patterns, or you might recognize yourself in only one. These behavior patterns all stem from the same longstanding negative conviction a woman has about herself (which, after reading this book, you will kiss good bye). However, the behaviors are very different from one another. Some solutions can be helpful across a broad range of types, while other strategies work better for a specific type. Where noted, you will benefit from specific solutions that are tied to your 'type' rather than generic encouragement.

This book includes an assessment so you can understand your specific type and get customized recommendations that will work best for YOU.

Curious? Ready to get know your type so you can find the solutions that match? Go take the assessment online now at **www.confidencetype.com**. You'll get a personalized and confidential report with your strengths and opportunities, and recommendations on which tools to get started with first in this book.

3. **Powered by Psychology** - Have you ever had the thought, "I've done so much work on myself, I'm brought so much value, how could I possibly *still* be here? How can I be doing this to myself, *yet again?*" No doubt, you've read all the blogs or been told by girlfriends, boyfriends, or family members to just stop criticizing yourself and begin believing in yourself more.

It's not that you lack the knowledge or the will. It's not that you don't already know the benefits to believing in yourself. Most of us already know what we 'should' be doing. It's a head scratcher when we just can't figure it out why in the heat of the moment, we don't always act as we intend to. This book gives you, finally, the explanation as to why this happens – along with a framework that makes it easy to understand how you can pivot and change those reactions, once and for all.

What's the surprising answer? At a high level: The approaches you've been using to try to build your confidence may very well be the exact tactics that are keeping you stalled at your existing confidence level, keeping you confused as to why you are so good at what you do but don't feel it in your bones . . . and if you haven't advanced according to your expectations, helping you question whether it's really you or is it bias. And arms you with awareness of the bias you are surrounded by so you can have success while being authentically you.

You will learn a repertoire of strategies that all work in concert to deconstruct your old way of doing things and support a lasting new way of confidence.

4. **Fast-acting strategies** – Every single strategy outlined in this book can be *learned within minutes and carried out within seconds*, if not instantaneously. So, forget the myth that it takes 10 years of stretch assignments to develop confidence, or 10 years of seeing clients to feel capable, or 10 years of therapy (like Woody Allen) to do something about your alleged 'issues.' Even if you were ever put down or felt that you didn't matter, you don't have to carry the burden of that unworthiness with you for the rest of your life.

The truth is, *you can start building rock solid confidence within seconds and see big changes in your life within minutes and days (or sooner, it all starts the moment you apply what you learn)*!

One final long-held myth is that you have to try really, *really* hard. "It's the journey, not the destination, you just have to keep at it," is our well-intentioned but vacant prop up to one another. As you'll begin to see in Chapter 3 and 4, trying doesn't necessarily work; in fact, it often backfires. Shortcuts are what have been proven to work best.

Beginning in Chapter 4, you'll learn the fastest way to build confidence, while the remainder of the book is filled with those time and energy saving shortcuts that will have you in a confident flow on demand! And you'll meet the women, just like you, who used them to their advantage to change their business and organization – and the world.

5. And Lasting ...

The tools you learn will not be the typical "Go to a conference and feel hyped up for a few days and then back to your old patterns"

I've been fortunate to speak at women's leadership networks at over 30 of the Fortune 500 companies and at many women's conferences around the world (including Healthcare Businesswomen's Association, Women in Cable and Telecommunications, Women's Leadership Exchange, Women Presidents Organization, Financial Women's Association and dozens of others). These forums serve as valuable networking forums and the bond is especially helpful for women who are often isolated as they make strides in male-dominated environments.

I sit there and listen with admiration to senior women in organizations tell the stories of amazing accomplishments. They share the story of their advancement and give heartfelt and helpful advice to audience members. "Take risks even though your plate is full," "tell your manager what you really want," and most importantly, "don't dwell on failures."

At business owner conferences, courageous women weave tales of rapid business growth, community awards, and how each entrepreneur can make her big impact in the world. They share the secret to their success as believing in her ideas, having the confidence to ask for the sale, and treating her employees with respect.

Audience members are mesmerized and inspired in the moment. They pledge to not apologize, to take risks, and to ask for what they want. However, in my experience, as those audience members return to their relentless list of demands, despite the best of intentions, they often revert to the comfort of their routine selves and make only small incremental changes, if they make any at all.

I hear from them that it's hard to overcome one's existing patterns. And for those who recognize it, the systematic penalties and exclusions in recruitment, retention, promotion, funding, resource allocation, etc. and all other means by which we build income and influence wears down our confidence and makes us question our hard-earned competence.

What I want is to move the needle. I want to equip you with the confidence tools to have the income, the influence, the impact that you have been put here to make. And contribute to positive evolution in your community, organization, and family. And to recognize and rise above bias, while doing any part that seems right for you to advocate for gender equality.

Of course, the number 1 thing I am asked at those conferences is… "how do I fix it?"

I want to move us from talking about it to doing it. This book is the HOW.

My clients often say to me "in the heat of the moment, your voice was in my mind; I thought of what you would tell me to say and do." So that's where I'll be for you - whispering in your ear about just how to build the skills you need. I'll help you finally bridge that gap between knowing what you *should do* and getting yourself to **actually do** it.

Part I:

Your "Now"

Chapter 1:
The Whole Picture (in Pictures):
The Case for Confidence

My father is a skillful ob-gyn with a sense of humor. When I was young, I used to love to listen to him come home and recount his patient interactions. Among his repertoire of 'greatest hit' quips was this: Patient: "Doctor, will my baby be a boy or a girl?" Dad: "Yes."

You could similarly answer "Yes" to any of the questions having to do with the issue of women and confidence and bias.

Are some women holding themselves back by having competence to speak up and play a bigger game but not consistently the confidence? "Yes."

Is there a clear gender bias such that capable women are passed over for promotion, hiring, funding, business growth, making their path to leadership and business growth harder? "Yes."

Is it because of women's biology or their socialization? "Yes."

Are men responsible; are women responsible? Can we all play a part in progress? "Yes."

Some of you might ask: Why are we trying to 'fix' the women? Instead, let's fix a patriarchal system based on traditionally masculine values and accept new forms of leadership that include women's styles.

To that I would answer: My first book, *Success under Stress*, was based on the idea that you only feel stress when aspects of a situation are out of your control. The mantra of that book is "Be Impeccable for your 50%", meaning control what you can control and be effective at what you can control.

Each woman's 50% part is to be ready: ready for promotion, ready to speak in front of the room, ready to call herself an expert and become skilled at 'selling' and marketing herself.

Each woman's part is to spend her precious time in the service of the contribution she wants to make and taking care of herself, not wearing herself thin, beating herself up, and needlessly over-preparing.

Each woman's part is to have awareness to not internalize or perpetuate the messages to be perfect or to not avoid risks that come from the pressures of her socialization. It's to know how to detach from the frustrations in the face of bias and then know effective ways of advocating for herself. And where she has energy and feels called to do so, to participate in changing the conversation that this is what it means to be a woman.

And it's the part of the stewards our culture – leaders, parents, politicians, educators, funders, Diversity and HR professionals, clergy, authors, media, etc. – to be intentional about the sub-cultures that are created in each family, team, company, community, state, and country. It's incumbent upon each of us in our current roles as influencers (or to get into roles as influencers) to use our awareness of inequality to change hearts, minds, and policies. To use our confidence to rise above pervasive bias by speaking up, influencing... and not perpetuating it ourselves.

If you are eager to get the tools to have confidence when it counts, feel free to skip right to Chapter 2. Otherwise, in this chapter I provide some research that provides context for the rest of the book. With these infographics, I aim to give a basic background of why a book about women and confidence in these times. And especially to provide a reference point for some of the ideas in the book about moments that count – distinguishing if it's me or is it bias (or both?) so you act effectively in the situation.

WHY CONFIDENCE?

INCOME	EXECUTIVE PRESENCE AND INFLUENCE	SUCCESS
Confidence increases Income over the course of your Career; Attracts Funding	(Confidence comprises 79% of a woman's "Gravitas")	More Productive, Achieve More; A Top 10 talent of successful Entrepreneurs

[1] http://www.afk.com/news/policy/industrial-relations/lifelong-confidence-rewarded-n-bigger-pay-packets-2012127-jh1?#ix3z42BOutr00
[2] Executive Presence, S.A. Hewlett, HarperBusiness, 2014; http://www.cbsnews.com/news/study-better-to-be-confident-than-right/
[3] http://www.gallup.com/businessjournal/173387/why-high-confidence-crucial-entrepreneurs.aspx; http://www.gallup.com/businessjournal/168623/talents-drive-entrepreneurial-success.aspx; http://www.babson.edu/Academics/centers/blank-center/global-research/diana/Documents/diana-project-executive-summary-2014.pdf
[4] Mindset, by Carol Dweck
[5] http://99u.com/articles/32306/are-confident-people-more-productive; http://faculty.haas.berkeley.edu/lyons/overconfidenceandvalue.pdf
[6] https://hbr.org/2016/01/how-age-and-gender-affect-self-improvement

Confidence is key regardless of gender. The greater your confidence, the more you earn, the more you succeed, the more you influence. Even your social life success is more dependent on confidence than on competence.

WOMEN AND CONFIDENCE

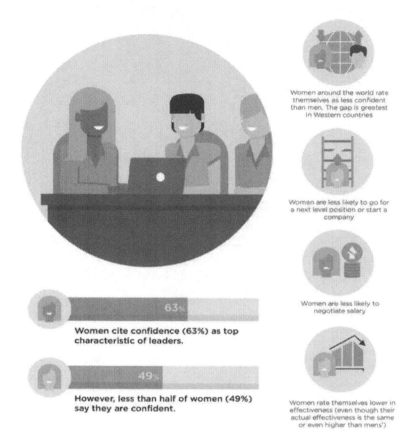

Women around the world rate themselves as less confident than men. The gap is greatest in Western countries

Women are less likely to go for a next level position or start a company

Women are less likely to negotiate salary

Women cite confidence (63%) as top characteristic of leaders.

However, less than half of women (49%) say they are confident.

Women rate themselves lower in effectiveness (even though their actual effectiveness is the same or even higher than mens')

[1] "Moving Women Forward Into Leadership Roles", KPMG.com/womensleadership;
[2] Bleidorn, W., Arslan, R. C., Denissen, J. J. A., Rentfrow, P. J., Gebauer, J. E., Potter, J., & Gosling, S. D. (2015, December 21). Age and Gender Differences in Self-Esteem—A Cross-Cultural Window. Journal of Personality and Social Psychology. Advance online publication. http:// dx.doi.org/10.1037/p-sp00000078
[3] Hewlett Packard internal study
[4] http://www.nber.org/papers/w18511#fromrss
[5] http://psycnet.apa.org/psycinfo/2014-15222-001/

When I told the head of a women's leadership network I was training the topic of this new book she said: "It's an epidemic. This is the #1 topic for the women in our office".

When I told the organizer of a women business association the topic before I spoke at their conference, she said: "I hear this every day from our members"

When I have given speeches on this issue, women flock to me afterwards saying how much they resonated with ideas.

Women recognize the importance of confidence. When asked about the most important skills needed to advance in 2015, Leadership and Confidence were tied at #1 amongst a large survey of professional women (KPMG.com/womensleadership).

Women across the board self report lower confidence than men, and this effect is greater in Western countries where women are more actively compared to men for salary, advancement, and potential. Though women are ambitious and actively seeking degrees, starting businesses, and seeking leadership roles, women are less likely to ask for or raise their hand for a next level position. It remains to be understood to what degree this is due to women's own doubt and to what extent it has to do with the way the qualifications are posted or the diminished control an upper role would afford her. Women perceive themselves as less capable than they are objectively, revealing a bias in self rating. One could describe this bias as follows: women are like Olympic gymnastics judges – they expect themselves to achieve a perfect 10 and deduct points for each perceived flaw (whereas we could anecdotally joke that men give themselves points for each thing they do right).

BIOLOGICAL/COGNITIVE REASONS FOR WOMEN'S CONFIDENCE

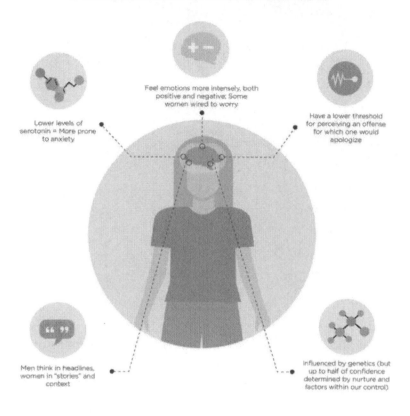

Feel emotions more intensely, both positive and negative; Some women wired to worry

Lower levels of serotonin = More prone to anxiety

Have a lower threshold for perceiving an offense for which one would apologize

Men think in headlines, women in "stories" and context

Influenced by genetics (but up to half of confidence determined by nurture and factors within our control)

[1] The Confidence Code, Claire Shipman and Katty Kay: http://www.ncbi.nlm.nih.gov/pubmed/29889486
[2] The Female Brain, LouAnn Brizendine.
[3] http://www.scientificamerican.com/podcast/episode/women-apologize-more-frequently-the-10-09-25/
[4] Cracking the Boys Club Code, Michael Johnson.

Men and women have many similarities and differences in their biology and cognition (and any studies of gender based biology are by definition generalizations.) There is probably more within gender than across gender variation, but it can be helpful to know that one's biology may set a woman up for certain behavioral responses that without this knowledge she could self blame.   Women feel emotions more intensely, both positive and negative. They are more likely to have gene and neurotransmitter patterns with lower levels of the 'happy' brain chemicals and make them more prone to focus on negative possibilities.

Women's brains have features that make them more likely to read the interpersonal effects of others behavior. These biological features are both competitive advantages and disadvantages in a work world – they make many women more empathic, sensitive to risk, and emotionally intelligent (which are traits associated with successful leadership in the current era and values of progressive companies). They also bring a level of intensity of emotion and personal connection to the work that has previously been unfamiliar in male-dominated workplaces. As you will see in the Infographic on gender bias, men are often lauded for their emotional displays in the workplace ('he's passionate') whereas women are penalized for displays of emotion ('she's emotional')

The hope for this book is that you learn tools to recognize and rise above emotionality from situations where it is caused by your own personal concerns, but to express passion effectively where warranted and inspiring.

Though genes that get expressed in the display we call "Confidence" have a large component that is inherited, up to half of confidence is determined by nurture and growth abilities within our control).

SOCIALIZATION REASONS FOR WOMEN'S CONFIDENCE

Women's often socialized to define worth by relationships

Boys are socialized to get skinned knees and endure teasing; Girls socialized to be "nice, smart, and compliant"

Girls are socialized with pressures to look and act perfect; Are 25% more prone to perfectionism

Girls are encouraged to believe abilities are innate and unchange-able, Boys encouraged to persist in effort.

1 KPMG, 2015
2 http://www.nytimes.com/2016/02/21/opinion/sunday/why-do-we-teach-girls-that-its-cute-to-be-scared.html?_r=0
http://www.slate.com/articles/life/family/2011/04/nervous_nellies.html
3 https://www.psychologytoday.com/blog/the-science-success/201101/the-trouble-bright-girls
4 The Confidence Code, Claire Shipman and Katty Kay
5 http://www.telegraph.co.uk/news/uknews/6634686/Women-worry-about-their-bodies-252-times-a-week.html
6 http://everydayfeminism.com/2014/05/feminism-and-anxiety/
7 http://www.nytimes.com/2013/09/08/education/harvard-case-study-gender-equity.html?hp&_r=1

Now that society is shining a lens on the gap between women's competence and confidence, many women are reflecting on their socialization and how it affects their decision making to this day. Ideas that some have coalesced around are the following:

a) the "skinned knee" idea – where boys are taught to venture forth, make mistakes, and deal with skinned knees, whereas girls are taught to be 'nice', compliant, smart, obedient and not pushed to apply themselves outside of their comfort zone;

b) the 'rough and tumble' idea whereby boys tease one another and develop a thick skin, whereas girls are socialized to build consensus and prioritize relational harmony; as adults, women are less familiar with a male dominated environment of politicking and non-respectful disagreement, it wouldn't be the culture they would create on their teams.

c) the 'attribution bias' whereby girls are taught they can control their behavior and thus attribute flaws to their innate abilities, whereas boys are expected to be less controlled and attribute success to their efforts;

d) the 'taking care vs taking charge' dichotomy where by girls are taught to 'take care' of others and look good for them, whereas boys are taught that it's gender congruent to act agentic and 'take charge'. Despite many well-meaning parents' efforts to provide gender neutral socialization, the messages are so pervasive and in some cases so biologically engrained that one can see girls' early confidence start to retreat in the early teen years if not before.

[What this discussion does not include is that boys are in crisis in their own way. By not being taught to be controlled, they are lagging in educational system, and more prone to deal with feelings through avoidant behaviors such as alcohol or drugs, or stonewalling which can lead to health conditions].

GENDER BIAS EXISTS

WOMEN'S COMPETENCE IS HIGH:

 When 30% of senior leaders are women, bottom line profit and employee engagement increase

 Women rated as more effective leaders

 Tipping point: 3 women on a board increases bottom line profit 63%

 Women make better investment decisions

 Women Executives Make Venture-Backed Companies More Successful

[1] http://www.pike.com/publications/wo/wp16-3.pdf
[2] Journal of Applied Psychology, Vol 99(6), Nov 2014, 1129-1145 http://dx.doi.org/10.1037/a0036751
[3] http://www.catalyst.org/system/files/The_Bottom_Line_Corporate_Performance_and_Womens_Representation_on_Boards.pdf
[4] https://www.insidehighered.com/news/2014/04/24/study-finds-faculty-members-are-more-likely-respond-white-males-others
[5] http://www.goldenseeds.com/content/PDFs/WomenPE_report_final.pdf

GENDER BIAS EXISTS

RATINGS OF WORK BY WOMEN IS LOWER:

RATED

Women's work is rated higher than and accepted more than men's when gender of the worker is not known. When gender of worker is revealed, women are rated lower than men.

HIRED

When exact resumes are presented with a clear male and female name, the male candidate is chosen x times more often

EVALUATED

Women have less influence; their contributions judged less positively; they are given credit less often

LESS OPPORTUNITY

Professors respond more often to outreach for mentorship from white males than women and minorities.

PAID

Pay gap grows as women are promoted; Gap is largest for women who are perceived to put family over work

¹ https://www.technologyreview.com/s/600812/female-coders-are-more-competent-than-males-according-to-a-new-study/
² cited by Shelley Correll, 2012 Minimizing Gender Bias in the Workplace https://www.youtube.com/watch?v=eblM3Xwco
³ summarized by Shelley Correll, 2012 Minimizing Gender Bias in the Workplace https://www.youtube.com/watch?v=eblM3Xwco
⁴ https://www.insidehighered.com/news/2014/04/24/study-finds-faculty-members-are-more-likely-respond-white-males-others
⁵ Psychol Sci. 2015 Nov;26(11):1751-61. doi: 10.1177/0956797615588739. Epub 2015 Sep 18. http://www.ncbi.nlm.nih.gov/pubmed/26386015
⁶ http://features.thecrimson.com/2015/senior-survey/
⁷ https://hbr.org/2015/11/how-the-gender-pay-gap-widens-as-women-get-promoted

The evidence is incontrovertible: women are 'value-add' and bring bottom line improvements in every position of power they enter. When the number of women entering senior leadership ranks or board positions of a corporation/start up increase, the bottom line profits of a company also increases. Women are highly effective at making investment decisions, gaining sales, and leading teams – outperforming men on most metrics and ratings.

Contrast these black and white quantitative findings with the evidence of gender bias. When ratings of performance are made while aware a performer's gender, women are rated lower than men. Women are rated, evaluated, and paid less than men across the board. They are mentored and sponsored and funded less often than men.

PROVEN GENDER BIASES

Leadership and Likeability Bias
Men who talk more and act like leaders are more likeable, women who talk more and act like (masculine traits of) leaders are less likeable.

Performance Attribution Bias
Women are given less credit for successful outcomes and blamed for failure.

Emotional Display Bias
Women are penalized for displays of emotion whereas men gain stature.

Motherhood Penalty /Parental bias
Parents (mothers and fathers) receive lower performance ratings, lower salaries, and increased scrutiny in job performance.

Prove it Again Bias
Promotion criteria based on future potential for men and past performance for women. Women have to provide more evidence of competence to be considered as competent as male colleagues.

[1] Victoria Brescoll, https://hbr.org/visual-library/2015/03/percent-of-u-s-women-in-stem-who-report; Mckinsey and LI, 2015, page 23 citation 10
[2] http://fortune.com/2014/08/26/performance-review-gender-bias/ https://pss.sagepub.com/content/19/3/268 abstract; get fortune performance reviews article
[3] https://hbr.org/visual-library/2015/03/percent-of-u-s-women-in-stem-who-report
Williams book what works for women at work: http://gender.stanford.edu/news/2014/what-works-women-work#athash.r9Dvi04Vi.dpuf
http://www.kent.ac.uk/news/society/5184/male-managerial-potential-rated-better-than-female-track-record
[5] https://www.evernote.com/shard/s120/n-
U3310977/d4aee16f-5bd7-4cef-8bba-cbaa59bd4086/?csrfBusterToken=U%3Dcblc01%3AP%3D%2F%3AE%3D1534ee4d089%3A5%3De362cf37eb4021
b6b8e3c6e70bfe7011
[6] Mckinsey/LI study, http://www.hbs.edu/faculty/conferences/2013-w50-research-symposium/Documents/correl.pdf
[7] https://hbr.org/2015/11/how-the-gender-pay-gap-widens-as-women-get-promoted

Throughout evolution, human beings have been socialized to associate agentic or leadership behaviors as a masculine trait. Women have entered into leadership positions in the business, political, and athletic world relatively recently in the course of evolution and this collective, systematic 'unconscious bias' toward 'leaders = men" remains quite active.

The **Performance/Likeability Bias**: We hold mental models of leaders as "male": when men act like a leader they are seen as "confident". Women are pressured to act in feminine roles and are penalized when act like 'leaders.' Yet women face the so-called **'tightrope' bias** (akin to the challenges of Goldilocks) where they have little wiggle room between being 'too masculine/coming on too strong and being 'not assertive enough/too nice".

When a woman asserts herself, or negotiates, she faces a social penalty (is called aggressive or out for herself and rated lower); when a man does the same he is seen as confident. When CEOs lead meetings, male CEOs who speak up are rated high as leaders, and women CEOs who speak up are rated lower. Women are penalized for displays of emotion whereas men gain stature. Of critical feedback in performance reviews about personality or emotion-related traits, 76% directed at women, and only 2% at men.

The issue seems to be one of 'role congruity' – when a woman acts in accordance with 'feminine roles' (i.e., leadership behaviors that are nurturing and collaborative) she is rated highly, but when she acts agentic she is rated lower (because she is acting with more masculine traits). This constrains women's leadership behavior options and gives added stress of the 'double bind'.

The **"Prove it Again" Bias**: Promotion criteria for men based on future potential whereas promotion criteria for women based on past performance. Women have to provide MORE evidence of competence to be considered as competent as their male colleagues (finally proving the age old saying that the famous dancer "Ginger Rogers had to do everything that Fred Astaire did but backwards and in high heels").

Parental Bias: Though we have traditionally associated parental bias with women, research now indicates that both men and women who make work related decisions or requests based on parenting needs are perceived as less committed and receive lower pay.

Emotional Display Bias: Men who display emotion in the workplace are considered "passionate/charismatic" and are lauded for it. Women who display emotion in the workplace are considered "emotional" and face a penalty in social and performance ratings.

EFFECTS OF GENDER BIAS

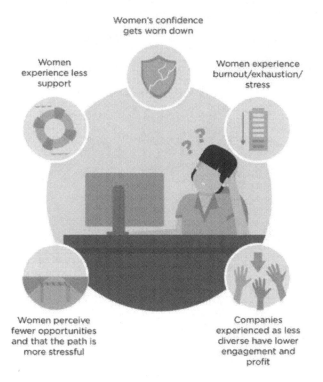

[1] Bain and Company, 2015
[2] McKinsey and Lean In, 2015
[3] https://hbr.org/visual-library/2015/05/why-women-report-a-drop-in-confidence-about-work-opportunities
[4] http://spp.sagepub.com/content/early/2015/02/24/1948550615576637.abstract
[5] http://www.gallup.com/businessjournal/166220/business-benefits-gender-diversity.aspx

The effects of gender bias are clear: Within 2 years of entering the workforce and encountering bias, women's confidence plummets (whereas men's' stays the same or rises). Women perceive fewer opportunities, and less support. All of these phenomena culminate in the finding that women's #1 perceived barrier to advancement is now 'stress/pressure', moving into the top spot beyond the traditional barrier of 'how to do it all' work-life challenges (McKinsey, 2015).

When gender bias persists, everyone loses. Diversity of all kinds improves team performance, and opens up new markets and innovation. Companies who are experienced as being as less diverse and providing fewer opportunities for diverse talent have lower overall engagement.

Chapter 2:
From Confusion to Clarity:
Know your Confidence Type

You've produced results over and over again. You have numerous accomplishments to point to. Your clients, your manager, your boyfriends, your girlfriends have all complimented you. For years, you've known you be "should" be less critical of yourself, and you've probably tried.

Why then do you still have moments where you self-criticize and hold yourself back? Why do you judge and compare yourself to others? Why do you still react defensively and take things personally?

Why might Groundhog Day happen any day of the year for you?

What I discovered in my research at Harvard Medical School is that the ways you've been trying to build confidence might be the very things that are keeping you at your current level of confidence. Keeping you 'doing it again'.

Let me explain with the following diagram. In order to be a confident leader or a growing entrepreneur, you must act from a place of confidence within. You need to feel secure in your own self so you can make bold decisions and believe you deserve a seat at the table (or head the table). You need to feel worthy in your role so you will speak up, and take action to pursue bigger opportunities. That inner experience of confidence, security, and worthiness is the 'holy grail', where confidence from within leads to success. (Diagram 1) This state is portrayed in the lower right hand corner.

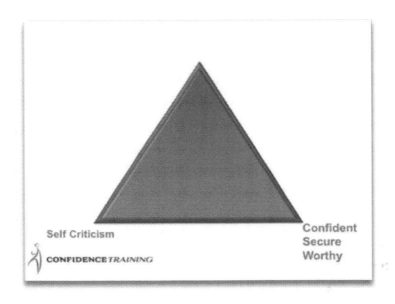

Self Criticism

Confident
Secure
Worthy

CONFIDENCE TRAINING

Diagram 1

The lower left corner represents the way you evaluate yourself at any given moment. If you criticize yourself to any extent, have a doubt, judge, compare, or question yourself, that inner experience will be reflected as "Self-Criticism/Doubt." Even if you have been praised, have helped other people, and have accomplishments to point to, if you do still have a pocket of doubt or self-criticism, it means you are not consistently acting from a place of rock solid confidence.

You might 'know in your mind' you are good at what you do but you don't always 'feel it in your bones'

However, we are all motivated to get to the lower right hand corner. It's the purpose of our lives to feel successful and self-expressed. Your negative voice will even set you up to try to get to that lower right hand corner. You'll do whatever it takes to get there. Typically, we don't connect the 'negative voice' to the actions it sets us up to take, but this chapter will help you create that awareness.

From having coached and trained over 19,000 people in 17 countries around the world, I see the pattern shown in Diagram 2:

You'll act toward other people (depicted as the arrow up the left hand side of the triangle), **in order to get other people to act toward you** (depicted as the arrow down the right hand side of the triangle), **so that you can feel in that confident place. Your time, energy and attention goes toward managing other people's perceptions. You'll involve other people in your efforts to create a desired experience inside yourself.**

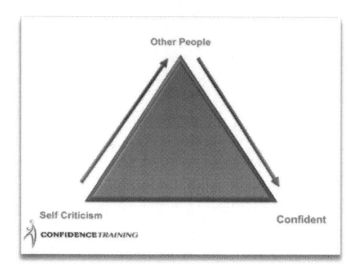

Diagram 2

There are 3 common variations on this pattern. Each pattern aims to get you from self-doubt to a sense of confidence. These patterns will explain behaviors that you may not even have realized were connected to your confidence or understood how they might 'get in your way'. Notice if you recognize yourself (or anyone you work with or live with) in one, two, or all 3 of these patterns.

Pattern #1: Seeking Approval

You put your time, energy, and attention into getting other people to think well of you (*If you follow along with Diagram 3, your behaviors are "up the left hand side of the triangle"*). You do these actions in the hope that others will approve, validate, reassure, or compliment you (*the behaviors you hope others will respond with are down the right hand side of the triangle.*) Why? When you don't feel fully confident within yourself, you aim to get other people to think well of you so you can see yourself through their eyes. In this way, you borrow their confidence. The strategy is as follows: " My boss/client says I'm doing a really good job, so I must be worthy of being in the role/ I must be good at what I do." You try to boost your confidence through the way they approve, validate, and reassure you.

The essence of this pattern is behaving to *get* other people's approval from the outside... so you can feel valuable on the inside.

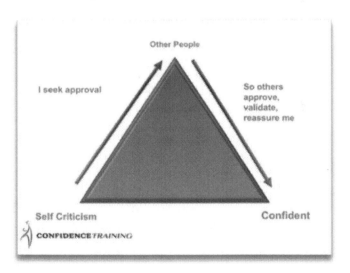

Diagram 3

Consult the checklist on the next page and put a checkmark by the behaviors that you notice yourself doing regularly (or at least in the moments that count). Put a special star * by the behaviors that you do very often or you would say characterize your behavior.

Performer: Seeking Approval Behaviors

- *Please your boss or team members (or romantic partner) by saying what they want to hear instead of your real thoughts or point of view.*

- *Over-prepare for meetings to make sure everyone thinks you are smart.*

- *Say yes when you would like to say no, to please or live up to expectations*

- *Ask other people's opinions for reassurance even when you are qualified to make a decision on your own.*

- *Talk a lot, over-justifying yourself so others think you are smart.*

- *Take things personally – "react," get defensive or feel undervalued because you are monitoring how much you are valued.*

- *Allow others to pass low level responsibilities to you – give endlessly and rarely ask for anything in return. Afterwards, feel resentful.*

- *Take credit for wins to get recognized by others OR don't take credit where you should.*

- *Compliment others in a way that 'fishes' for compliments back.*

- *Don't delegate as much as you should because you don't trust other people to produce as perfect a deliverable as you would.*

- *Spend excessive time redoing an email in order to be well-evaluated.*

- *Take care of others before taking care of yourself; try to rescue others (in the hopes that they will appreciate you/ show you "love").*

- *Justify all you have done in order to get a compliment (and feel resentful if you don't feel recognized).*

- *Worry/fuss over how you look, maybe changing your outfit several times.*

- *Control or micromanage other people.*

- *Take blame and immediately apologize to prevent others being mad at you, try to appease others*

- *Keep yourself busy doing favors for other people. Feel you have to say yes to every request and expectation of you (Note: I'm a big fan of being generous, a team player, or an active connector in your network — I am referring to when you go too far and don't exercise or don't complete your own work because you are seeking others' appreciation.)*
- *Become too much like your romantic partner/ lose yourself so you will be liked*
- *(Your 'approval-seeking' behavior here)_____*

But shouldn't I care about what my manager and clients think about me?

Yes, it is appropriate to care what your manager, peers, and clients think about the service/role/result they are paying you to deliver. You want to be open to their feedback so you can always improve your contribution. The distinction is that you want to be confident in your own *self-worth*, and then use their feedback to help you improve *your service or your performance*. **You want to take in their feedback as it relates to your work, not about your worthiness as a human being.** You want their approval to be the cherry on top of the ice cream sundae, not the sundae itself. You don't want others' feedback about you to be the only supply line to your "emotional" oxygen, you want to have a secure base of 'owning your value' from within (otherwise it's too dangerous to have your supply line threatened so you will keep up behaviors to please others). Also, you want to have a sense of security in yourself so that when you are complimented, it has a match within your self-schema and can stick (rather than doing all that effort to get complimented then not even taking it in.)

Here's an example of this Confidence Type.

Linda: The Performer/Pleaser

Linda is part of a sales team in a large financial firm. She is sensitive to how much she is being valued or not by her manager. Linda wants to grow her clientele and wants to be promoted so she cares A LOT what her manager and networking community think about her. When she wins a client account, she tries to manufacture an opportunity to run into her manager in the hall and tell him about it. When he responds by saying, "I knew you could do that; that's why I hired you," she's over the moon. When she gives him the good news and he gives a tepid response, she's deflated.

She's a valuable member of her networking group, yet she frequently spends so much time doing favors for other people that she doesn't have time to finish her own work, much less have time to get to the gym. She over-prepares for client meetings so they'll *never* ask her a question that she can't answer. Even though she knows more about the business than just about anyone, she'll often ask others for input into decision-making instead of just trusting herself. Linda is always very aware of who is getting which resources – she shares the office with a male colleague who has the 'bigger fish' clients and is always going to events such as ballgames and dinners with them. Linda is resentful and wants the confidence to have more influence and income.

What to notice about Linda's behavior: She is 'other oriented.' She weighs her boss's opinion of her more heavily than her own. Her energy is drained by efforts to get boosting feedback from her boss, and she is deflated if he doesn't give her what she seeks. She monitors the other people in the office. I once heard a pithy way of describing this in a 360-performance review I did for a client, her manager said: "I would like to see her be more about the work and less about the noise about the work."

Pattern #2: Preventing Disapproval.

The second pattern is the opposite of the first. Whereas the first pattern aims to 'get other's approval,' in this pattern, your behavior is aimed at preventing other's disapproval. To the extent you have doubt or self-criticism, what becomes very important for you? That's right, making sure nobody else knows about your perceived weakness. So, what are you going to do? You act toward other people to prevent them from disapproving, criticizing, rejecting you, etc.

In this pattern, you will act *(up the left hand side of the triangle)* by holding back, not speaking up, not asking, avoiding conflict, etc. You do this to prevent other people from criticizing, rejecting, disapproving, giving negative feedback *(down the right hand side of the triangle*; See Diagram 4).

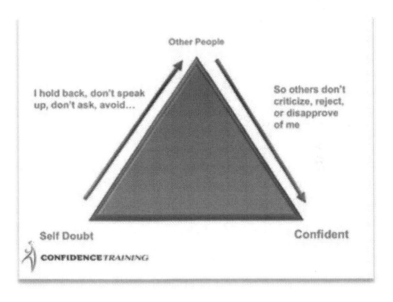

Diagram 4

The essence of this pattern is holding yourself back to hold onto the confidence you've built. You don't pursue or take advantage of existing opportunities to *prevent* other people's negative feedback. The intent is to hold onto the respect that you have earned and not lose it or have it be threatened by others' judgments. You prevent negative feedback because if exposed to others' criticisms, you don't trust yourself to have an independent evaluation of yourself. In your history, once you hear critiques or get a response that could be perceived as rejecting, you've believed their input, causing you to doubt, question, or criticize yourself.

If you are concerned that others might judge your contribution as mundane, not value add, "stupid," "not smart enough," etc. you will simply not give them an opportunity to criticize you or evaluate you negatively. You might procrastinate getting started, or finishing the project, thinking to yourself, "Who am I to raise my hand for that stretch opportunity?" "Who am I volunteer to give that speech or to get up and represent my company or my group in front of other people?" "Who am I to raise my fees, or ask for a salary? Better to keep expectations of me low so that I can guarantee that I can meet them." So, you stay in your comfort zone and don't stretch yourself.

This is the pattern I demonstrated when I said "No" to the White House!

Consult the checklist on the next page and put a checkmark by the behaviors that you notice yourself doing regularly (or at least in the moments that count). Put a special star * by the behaviors that you do very often or you would say characterize your behavior.

Protector: Preventing Disapproval Behaviors

— *Don't speak up even when you have valuable info or perspectives to share, instead worrying "what will they think?"*

— *Not speak up or act for fear of making a mistake*

— *Stay in your comfort zone (using behaviors with which you've already had success rather than putting yourself out for a next level opportunity, starting a new service, trying out a new niche, raising your hand for greater responsibility, volunteering to lead a group, etc.).*

— *Sell yourself short on fees or not ask for higher salary (so you can keep others' expectations of you low).*

— *Not take risks.*

— *Get nervous about presentations/put off preparing out of worry you will be judged.*

— *Not ASK for the business, for time with important people, for resources that would help you do your job, for a raise, etc.*

— *Not go after bigger fish clients or projects.*

— *NOT take action on a next career step or a desired action to move your business forward because you don't feel "ready" (e.g., procrastinate writing a book, speaking at an event, or reaching out about job opportunities)*

— *Not push back or stand your ground with senior leaders or a difficult client.*

— *Stay in your comfort zone of busy work— carrying out your job instead of stretching to come up with bold ideas or act like a leader.*

— *Procrastinate. Talk about but not doing things essential for your career*

— *'Freeze' when you are questioned by senior management or high level decision makers.*

— *Worry about reaching the next level of success because of increased expectations.*

- *Don't negotiate where appropriate*
- *Avoid confrontations and soft pedal, afraid others won't like you or be angry with you.*
- *Not initiate or accept opportunities to speak or lead, thinking "who am I to…"*
- *Wait to start a new initiative or 'go for it' until 'more prepared' or more confident.*
- *Tolerate others' negative behavior or substandard performance, worried you won't be able to negotiate to get a replacement.*
- *Not initiate contact to someone you like in your personal life*
- *Not share your full self or be vulnerable out of concern you will be rejected or found 'not loveable'*
- *(Your Disapproval Preventing Behavior)*

————————————————————————

Here's an example of someone who tries to Prevent Disapproval:

Sonya: The Protector

Sonya is a solopreneur who holds herself back. She coaches entrepreneurs and executives on time management. Her clients believe she does a great job, and she wants to grow her business. Sonya has a great personality and has some excellent ideas to get before audiences as a speaker. However, whenever she thinks about becoming more publicly visible, she discounts her abilities. "Who am I to be the 'expert' in front of the room? I'm not ready. What if I get up there and flop?"

Doubt and fear creep in as she tries to grow her business. For example, she wants to raise her fees but hasn't done so in order to keep client expectations of her low. She's spent months rebranding her website, painstakingly writing and rewriting the 'About' and 'Services' sections because they're never good enough. She wants to take on an associate to help her service her clients but doesn't trust herself to earn enough. She was asked by a friend to appear on a popular local radio show, finally saying 'yes' – but only at her friend's insistence and not without freak-outs and hesitations. Excited about the interview prospect, she procrastinated on her script because she was nervous about being judged.

What to notice about Sonya's behavior: Sonya really wants to grow her business but she is "playing not to lose" instead of playing to win. She's judging herself before she'll ever give other people an opportunity to judge her.

Pattern #3: Looping Self/Other Criticism.

The first two patterns were about the time, energy, and attention you put into managing others' perceptions of you. The first pattern was about seeking approval; the second pattern was about preventing disapproval – all so that you could try to get that feeling of confidence within. In this third pattern, you put time, energy, and attention into your own critical perception of yourself. (See Diagram 5) You create a negative loop of pressure and self-criticism in order to live up to an internal ideal or perceived expectation from others.

This self-criticism can be intended to help you improve yourself – indeed, you might wonder how you could 'keep your edge' if fear of humiliation doesn't motivate you to over-prepare. You might think that your focus on what you 'did wrong' will help you do it better next time. But usually your self-criticism is not constructive feedback, so it inevitably keeps you feeling defeated. You might be concerned that if you are not 'perfect' things you will disappoint/threaten a relationship or will fall apart and be 'your fault'.

One thing to be aware of is if you impose this criticism on other people, they might also feel 'never enough'.

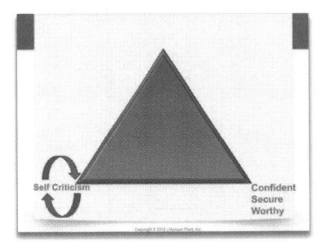

Diagram 4

Consult the checklist on the next page and put a checkmark by the behaviors that you notice yourself doing regularly (or at least in the moments that count). Put a special star * by the behaviors that you do very often or you would say characterize your behavior.

Perfectionist/Criticizer: Looping Self Criticism

— *Magnifying mistakes (You notice a mistake that others might not even see and you magnify it into a total failure).*

— *Black and White views: Any imperfection makes you a failure.*

— *You judge yourself and beat yourself up*

— *You always look at the gap. (You did nine things well but one could use improvement, and all you see is the one).*

— *You are never "good enough"*

— *Others are never "good enough" for you.*

— *Do- and re-do work until it's perfect (except it never is).*

— *You feel embarrassed or ashamed about something that wasn't perfect and it's hard to 'let it go' – you keep obsessing about it*

— *Speak to yourself in harsh terms ('you better not screw this up', "I'm an idiot!)*

— *Don't go for a next level opportunity unless it's 'no fail', assured you will succeed*

— *Quick to judgment*

— *Often think you are right (or else the opposite, that you are always wrong)*

— *Quick to take blame and see things as 'all your fault' and responsible*

— *Not enough self care, it doesn't feel comfortable doing nice things for yourself*

— *Your mind races, hard to have peace of mind*

— *(Your Self/Other Critical Looping Behavior)*

In short, the essence of this is being a criticizer and creating an attentional loop focused on the gap. You criticize yourself in the hopes of improving - but it's harsh and feels deserved, so little learning takes place. You might beat yourself up for mistakes, and get stuck in feelings of self-judging shame. This self-criticism loop might run in your head as you energetically perform well with the only consequence that it exhausts you. Or this critical voice might set you up to do any of the "seeking approval" or "preventing disapproval" behaviors in Patterns #1 and 2.

Here's an example of someone who Loops in Self Criticism:

Nikki: Perfectionist/Criticizer

Nikki is a mid-level manager of a large pharmaceutical company. She wins praise across the board for her ability to achieve goals while nothing falls through the cracks on her watch. She's a perfectionist – extremely smart and capable. Her focus is often on the details and, perhaps too often, her perspective is that she is one who is right. She's her own worst critic. Nikki perceives mistakes where others see none. Despite this, she spends the rest of the day rehashing her perceived shortcomings in her mind. Nikki is such a superstar that she was just tasked with leading a bigger project. Now she has to make a decision. She wants to go for it because she thinks she should be further ahead in her career, but she only wants to accept if she's positive she'll succeed. She seen as a 'go to' executor but it comes with a cost – she is considered to be highly demanding of her team. They can tell when she gets a harsh tone that she is not pleased with them and they feel a little dismissed.

Notice that Nikki is both hard on herself and on her team. Sometimes, a criticizer is only critical of herself and other times, she's a driver who also sees other people as 'not good enough.' Other people think she is a star and can't understand why she is so critical of herself.

Now it's YOUR turn. Time for you to identify which is your Type or Types. That way you know exactly what your pattern(s) is and which of the tools in the subsequent chapters will be the most useful for you. Some people have one clear behavior pattern; others show behaviors from more than one pattern.

What do I mean by a Confidence Type? We each have a characteristic way (or ways) of getting to that experience in the right-hand corner of confidence, security, worthiness. We each have a characteristic way of dealing with ourselves when we hear that internal negative voice. That behavior pattern has strengths and opportunities associated with it. It's helpful to be aware of YOUR pattern so you know where it's helping – and hurting – you. It's also helpful to be aware when you are doing these behaviors so you can use the solutions in part II of this book to rise above these patterns and get the confidence they are intended to achieve.

You might be only 1 type, or even relate to all 3. (Note: I have been ALL 3 types in my life, that's why I know them so well ;-)

It's important to know your type because common advice we read in blogs and shared amongst well-meaning friends might be wrong for your type and backfire. For example, if you are a Performer or Perfectionist, being told how great you are by your girlfriends over drinks will be a fun night out(!) but perpetuate your pattern of getting others' input in order to feel good inside. If you are a Perfectionist, being told to 'lower your expectations' just frustrates you (see Chapter 7 instead.) If you are a Protector, being told 'just believe in yourself', or 'try to always speak up within the first 5 minutes of the meeting' isn't going to get you over your entrenched hesitation (see Chapter 6 instead).

You can identify your type in the following two ways.

1) First, add up your checked items under patterns 1, 2, and 3 – especially tally the behaviors that you 'starred' with an * (These are the behaviors you do often or that characterize your pattern). Which category did you have the most of? That will give you a 'quick and dirty' idea of your primary 'type'. If you checked off a lot of behaviors in more than 1 type, that's a sign that your behaviors span more than 1 pattern. Which category did you have the second most often? That's your secondary category.

2) Second, a more accurate and interesting approach is to take the online assessment (**www.confidencetype.com**) It will present you with several common scenarios of 'moments that count' and allow you to indicate how you would respond. The assessment will do the calculation for you, and report your categories. It will provide you with a personalized, confidential report that describes the strengths and opportunities for each of your types. It will guide you to the strategies that are right for you to use right away.

(The online assessment also includes a 4th category, that of Confident Leader. This is the 4th type, the most effective and direct way of achieving confidence and security. You may already be showing this behavior in your daily life in a good number of situations. Yet from analyzing over 1200 assessment, **every assessment taker who is categorized Confident Leader also has some scenarios in which they show one of the other Confidence Type patterns in the 'moments that count'.** So, take the assessment and learn your behavior in the moments that count.)

The online version is also fun because it will tell you which celebrities you are similar to (and how they became confident!) Go take the online assessment now at **www.confidencetype.com**.

POINTS TO REMEMBER

- When you have doubt or self-criticism, you try to get to a place of confidence and worthiness by trying to manage other people's perceptions or over focusing on your own.
- Three behavior patterns that represent the differing ways people try to regulate confidence are:
  - Seeking Approval
  - Preventing Disapproval
  - Looping Self/Other Criticism
- Knowing your Confidence type can help you identify the strengths and opportunities in your type, and match you with specific solutions right for you.
- Even if you receive a Confident Leader type (because you act that way in situations more often than the other types), you still might act from one of the other Type patterns in moments when it counts. So, all the strategies in this book apply to you too!

NEXT STEPS

- Take the assessment to discover your type!
  http://www.confidencetype.com/
- Notice when you do the behaviors that are characteristic of your pattern so you can apply solutions in Part II of this book

Chapter 3:
From Your Present to Your Future: Understanding the "Why" Behind Your Patterns to Let Them Go

The three patterns of behaviors described in Chapter 2 are "Indirect ways" of trying to get that sense of confidence and feeling secure from within. What I mean by "Indirect Behaviors" is that your behaviors **involve** other people (or your thoughts about other people) in your effort to feel worthy inside. Your time, energy, and attention go toward managing other people's perceptions, monitoring what they will think, say, or do toward you.

You try to get approval from others in order to try to build up your self-evaluation, and borrow the compliments of others to try to convince yourself of your worth.

Or you hold back to prevent others' disapproval so you can hold onto the confidence you have.

Or you criticize yourself with the intent of improving, punishing, or raising standards for yourself or others.

As you can see from Diagram 5, these are "**Indirect**" ways of trying to get to a sense of confidence inside of you. You are directing your behavior toward managing other people's actual or perceived responses to you, not directly toward the result you want.

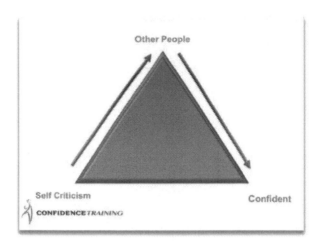

Diagram 5

Here's my big question to you: If these behaviors help you get a compliment, prevent you from being criticized, and make you motivated to improve your gaps in performance, *what's the problem? Why aren't these behaviors you should be doing?*

Here are seven ways that "Indirect" behaviors are problematic and interfere with your becoming the confident performer and person you want to be:

1. Indirect Behaviors are a quick fix: The effect is fleeting.

Managing people's perceptions does work to a degree. Yes, you may get a compliment, or relief from negative feedback. However, when you rely on Indirect Behaviors, confidence doesn't accumulate inside of you. For example, if your boss or a client tells you that you did a great job, you might feel 'over the moon' for an hour, a day, or maybe even a week if it's a hugely visible compliment. But if you don't derive your confidence from within, the effect will wear off. You'll have to go out and re-earn your sense of value by getting another compliment.

The effects of indirect behaviors are like a 'sugar high.' You get a temporary boost, or temporary relief from being criticized, or temporary examination of your flaws. But there is no substantial progress on building true belief in yourself. You will have to keep going to other people as the 'well' where you draw confidence from. You'll have to keep preventing disapproval in every meeting you go to. You will have keep beating yourself up – because these are the strategies you are using to get to a place of confidence. It's like being on a 'sugar cycle' where you have to keep eating more of it.

2. Indirect Behaviors win the small game but lose the big game.

Your Indirect Behaviors are about your 'small game' – the momentary concerns of doubt or fear, and feeling you need to control how you will be judged. They are not about your 'big game' – which is the contribution you are here to make, the legacy you want to leave, and the meaningful connections you want to make.

Your Indirect Behaviors are a way of fulfilling your universal basic human needs. We all have the need to feel loved and to prevent physical/emotional harm (in the form of criticism, rejection, abandonment, etc.). Indirect behaviors are aimed at fulfilling these basic needs, not at self-actualization where you put energy into fulfilling your highest potential and greatest contribution. *Indirect behaviors 'have gotten you here, but won't help you get there.'*

3. Indirect Behaviors are about you/your feelings not about the work.

I made the decision to decline the White House invitation based on my own feelings and evaluation about myself. It was "subjective," my own opinion of myself – which is often not even close to accurate! I didn't make that decision based on an objective analysis of the contribution I could have made to their programs empowering women.

If I was objective, I could have listed 10 research-based recommendations that would have added value to their existing programs. But my decision wasn't based on that. Indirect behaviors are about your opinions, not about the good work you can do.

Feelings of self-criticism or doubt put you into a situation of stress. They are associated with fear of others' judgments, shame or guilt about not being enough, anger at disappointment by others turned inwards. They create stress because you feel trapped in the negative moment and can't have the calm or proud feelings you desire. The part of your brain that was developed to sense threat becomes activated. When your brain has a choice between dealing with this sense of threat (i.e., fulfilling a basic need) or doing behaviors to build your business or lead effectively (i.e., a higher-level need), it will always prioritize taking care of the basic need. Your brain is wired to always prioritize efforts to gain confidence and do something to deal with your stressful feelings before it can turn attention to building your success.

4. Indirect Behaviors are controlling but make you feel out of control.

You can control your behaviors (up the left side of the triangle), but you cannot control others' thoughts and behaviors toward you (down the right side of the triangle). But you are making your ability to 'get to that right-hand corner' contingent on how others act toward you – you give away your power on a silver platter to whoever you're making your 'middleman' (top of the triangle).

Let's say your part in a project has been 'perfect', but your manager or business partner or difficult family member is having a bad day (or has limited emotional intelligence and doesn't notice you), then you won't get the approval or reassurance you were looking for. Then you might not feel confident because your supply line to that positive feedback wasn't flowing. With an Indirect approach, IT MATTERS how others think and act toward you because you need their input in order to feel secure inside. You put pressure on your "middleman" to give you what you need.

Even if you are a genuinely caring and service-oriented person, there is an aspect of your people-pleasing in which you "give to get." And if you don't get it, then you're going to try even harder to get it from them. You are going to beat yourself up or over-prepare more. Or you will hide out of fear even more.

5.   Indirect Behaviors are mental and exhausting.

I have nicknamed the Indirect Path approach as the "looking, waiting, hoping, and trying" path. That's a lot of energy going into managing other people! Indirect behaviors aren't about authentically feeling the good in you. Rather, they require you to calculate and control other people's responses – "How can I *get* my boss to notice my talents"; "How can I get my date to like me", "I have to do this presentation perfectly; someone important to my career will be in the room and they hold the key to my success." Or you might say to yourself "This presentation is full of mistakes; why did this happen, who's to blame, who noticed and what are they thinking…" It sets up a lot of pressure on yourself and others.

Indirect behaviors burn up mental and emotional energy. For example, Julie used to calculate how her boss would respond to certain leadership behaviors she was considering. Whenever a colleague didn't recognize her contribution to a meeting, she would blame others or feel undervalued. She often did the mental calculations comparing others' titles, or the ratio between how much others had contributed compared to her (and the credit each got). She would over-prepare for meetings, pressuring herself to "know everything" – to make sure nothing fell through the cracks and she wouldn't be caught having to say, "I don't know" and be judged unprepared. After she presented for senior management, she would do a thorough review, emphasizing her perceived flaws, wondering how others would report back to senior management about it, and trying to figure out how she could get a favorable report, etc. If people didn't catch on to her ideas quickly, she would be judgmental toward them and churn about how people should be as quick as her. You can hear the mental calculations. (Notice she has many behaviors characteristic of the Perfectionist/Criticizer Type) Indirect strategies are often mental, controlling and, in short, exhausting!

Plus, it's likely that you will shrug off any compliments received anyway. If you don't have a sense of yourself as deserving, compliments will lack a place to "stick onto" inside of you and will sluff off. Even if you do receive positive feedback for your hard work, you might not take it in - thus feeling empty of recognition, thinking you are not 'good enough,' and needing to keep doing high energy efforts to earn praise.

6. Indirect Behaviors are the long, slow way to get to your destination (and in the end, don't get you there).

Just eyeball the diagram to see that Indirect behaviors are the LONG way of getting where you want to go. They are the SLOW way. It's like having to climb up and around the mountain. You have to accumulate enough incremental progress from each sugar high moment until it would start to sink in. You have to waste hours and days beating yourself up on the path toward your goal of inner confidence. You also have to sink thousands of hours into managing the highs and lows of other people's perceptions and your reactions to them. This is the "It takes ten years of stretch assignments," or "Public speaking confidence only comes from years of practice" model.

And my final question is: Your Indirect Behaviors are exhausting, but do they help you arrive at the destination of rock solid confidence? Efforts to get results and not let anything fall through the cracks . . . to give to other people or calculate what you must do to hide from their criticism . . . or your own self-criticism . . . These are all aimed at getting confidence from within, but do you really get it?

No.

7.   Indirect behaviors create a vicious cycle.

The more you do them, the more you are *outsourcing your self-worth*. The more you do them, the more you have to keep doing them because you haven't built the inner resources for confidence within. That's why you might feel like you are on a treadmill.

That's why simplistic advice like "Believe in yourself, girlfriend," offers momentary encouragement but doesn't break the pattern. Or similarly, a well-meaning campaign for women to stop saying "I'm sorry" has brought helpful awareness around a discrete behavior but not a panacea for overall confidence building.

Is there something wrong with me if I use Indirect Behaviors?

NO! Indirect behaviors are completely normal. As infants, we are biologically hardwired to seek contingent responsiveness from caregivers.[i] Just as we need to breathe in oxygen to function and grow physically, we must take in "emotional oxygen" from caregivers in order to grow our self-esteem. Our parents' love and attention, teachers' evaluation and praise, and peers' approval and appreciation are the mechanisms by which we come to see ourselves – favorably or not. So, as you're growing up, it's natural to learn to see and know yourself through the eyes of others.

Indirect behaviors as adults are well-intended. Seeking a strong foundation of confidence is what you've been doing right. You've had good instincts to know you want to come from a place of confidence as a leader or entrepreneur. And these approaches worked in the short term.

Because we have learned to know ourselves through others' eyes, many of us continue this approach to regulating our confidence into adulthood. **The confidence needed for success comes by making the maturational shift to get confidence from within or from sources more within your control**. Only then will you possess the ability to feel confident in any situation, regardless of others' thoughts about you.

Women also are set up for confidence challenges by brain physiology that may predispose to negative emotion and rumination, social roles that emphasize a woman's value as being in relation to others, and looking perfect. And by continuous interaction with collective unconscious bias that begins in the early years of developing a belief in one's abilities to succeed in fields holding traditional stereotypes of males (see Chapter 1 for synopsis)

In this way, the pattern that you've been doing "right" has been limiting you. Or has been keeping you from having that confidence at the core which is the basis of your success.

From "Confidence Seeker" to "Confident Contributor"

Indirect Behaviors are variations of ways you "seek confidence." The motivations behind these three behavior patterns are to regulate your own self-regard – they are each a strategy to increase, maintain, or regain your sense of confidence.

These patterns are characteristic of you being a **"Confidence Seeker."**

You will never become secure and self-trusting if the approach you use to get there is Indirect – i.e., involving other people. If you are caught up in a vicious cycle of Indirect behaviors, you will never outgrow your current confidence and fulfill your potential.

This idea might even feel familiar to you if you have ever said to yourself that "too much time and energy is soaked up" dealing with this issue. Because the average professional has 30-100 projects on her plate, faces 139 emails a day, and has a never-ending to-do list[ii] – you are at a competitive disadvantage and are making your life more stressful if your time, energy, and attention are going toward Seeking Confidence.

What you want is to come from a place of confidence. Your mind is free of constraints. Your basic needs for 'emotional oxygen' are fulfilled, so your energies are directed toward higher order needs like learning and growing your success. ALL your time, energy, and attention goes toward making the contribution you were put here to make (and meaningful connections with people with whom you feel valuable and loved). That's what it means to be a **Confident Contributor**…

What's the Fix for Indirect Behaviors?

To shift from a Confidence Seeker to a Confident Contributor.

To get off the sugar highs and get on a protein diet.

To grow from approval seeking to accomplished.

To get out of automatic pilot and be authentically you.

To stop regrets and start results.

To end effortful and start effortless.

To shift from silent to speaking up.

The fastest way to build confidence is of course … to **Go Direct!**

Turn to the next chapter and let's get started…

POINTS TO REMEMBER:

- Indirect Behaviors:
  - Are intended to help you feel confident, but they backfire and outsource your confidence to others
  - Help you win the "small game but not your "big game"
  - Have a fleeting effect, are exhausting and create a vicious cycle where you have to keep doing them. They 'got you here by won't get you there."

NEXT STEPS

- If you haven't done so already, take the assessment and know your type(s) at **www.confidencetype.com**
- If you see how these Indirect patterns are costing you and want to jump right to my help with solutions, contact me at **sharon@sharonmelnick.com** or check out "C-school" (Confidence School **www.sharonmelnick.com/cwc**) or the Confident Influential Leader virtual coaching program **www.sharonmelnick.com/cil**.

Chapter 4:
From Indirect to Go Direct:
The Fastest Path to Confidence

"Very early in life, I figured out the most important relationship is with yourself. And if you figure that out, every other relationship you have is a plus, not a must!"

- Diane von Furstenberg, fashion pioneer and businesswoman

You're in a meeting and have something valuable to say? You . . . say it! (without the hesitation or inner debate).

You're asked why you haven't done something. You . . . stay poised and unruffled rather than taking it personally. You take a step back and calmly lead everyone to finish the project collaboratively.

A mistake was made. You . . . have the perspective to see the small part you played instead of taking blame for the whole thing. You learn the lesson and then get back to work with peace of mind.

An upcoming presentation on your calendar? You . . . get started working on it without debilitating anxiety of failure.

You started dating someone you really like. You...trust you are loveable and can be fully yourself.

You fall asleep at night thinking "I am who I am . . . and I'm ok with that!"

No, you won't need an alarm clock to wake up from this scenario; this isn't a dream. This is what life is like when you Go Direct! (Diagram 6)

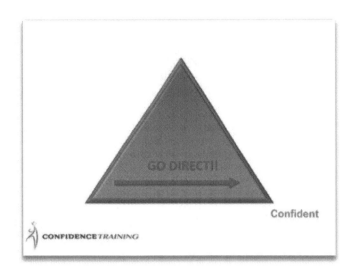

Diagram 6

Go Direct describes the behavior pattern in which you source your confidence from within, independently of others' evaluations of you. You feel filled by a sense of reward and satisfaction from your contributions. You know how to feel calm, at peace, and alive in your own body. You can access an experience of yourself as valuable 24/7/365, no matter who is around you or what they are thinking or saying. Thus, you can self-manage to be 'in your power.'

It enables you to have even more of the success you want without all the effort of the Indirect strategies. Instead of a 'borrowed' momentary boost, it's 'the real deal.' By not trying to control others, you feel in more control.

Go Direct is the summation of all the advice you've heard about how to be confident, encapsulated into one idea. Over and over, I've seen examples of how you get more of what you want with less effort.

In the subsequent chapters, you will learn practical strategies how to apply the idea of Go Direct. In order to 'get' the idea of Go Direct, here are the seven mindsets that characterize the Direct path. These will enable you to drop old behaviors in favor of new ones.

Intentional:

When your mode of operation is Indirect, you tend to over focus on what emotion is getting activated in you *now*. Caught in a crunch moment, your automatic strategy achieves the quickest way out of the discomfort and into that momentary feeling of confidence or relief. Or when you are caught up in regret about the past or worry about the future, you are not fully present to yourself in that moment and you don't see yourself of being in control of a powerful outcome – that's why you use an "Indirect" expedient strategy to at least get the best you can to get through the situation.

Go Direct is about being intentional. Intentional means "done or brought about of one's own will" – with freedom of choice, without external compulsion, from an awareness of an end to be achieved. You decide on the outcome you want to create (hopefully, this is what is in the best interest of all in the situation) and identify the experience you want to have. And then act "in the service" of that outcome. In this way, you shift from reactive to intentional.

You play a part in setting up the outcome you want. When your approaches are Indirect, you can feel 'jerked around' or on your heels because your ability to get needed responses is left up to how the other person is thinking or acting today. The way to get what you want in your life is to act with intention each and every moment in the service of creating it.

Proactive:

"Waiting" is Indirect. It's looking to others, waiting for their input, hoping they will give you permission or give you your desired internal experience.

Go Direct is encapsulated by this quote by Lynne Doughtie, U.S. Chairman and CEO, KPMG: "Own your career. Don't wait for someone to tap you on the shoulder and present an opportunity to you."

It can feel uncomfortable for women to take the initiative, utilizing behaviors that might be associated with being 'aggressive' (that's what leads to the gender incongruity penalty). We see this in everything from asking for a raise to women needing to be asked on average 9 times to run for office.

So, I'm not encouraging you to be aggressive; I'm encouraging you to be proactive – letting your manager know about your career aspirations and not expecting them (or your spouse) to read your mind. Not hoping that people from networking events will refer to you but rather inviting prospects to a speech you are giving, or providing them with the language to introduce other people to you.

A great example of being Proactive is the Rwandan women who took post-war reconstruction into their own hands and are seen as a major force behind the post-conflict successes.[iii] The idea was "we're not waiting for you fellas to make up." This was an example of Annie Lennox's song "Sisters are doin' it for ourselves!" One Rwandan woman started a 'peace basket' weaving initiative in which Tutsi and Hutu women came together to heal social wounds and earn money for emergency medical and security efforts. These efforts blossomed into advocacy at a governmental level and ultimately led to the adoption of a gender quota enshrined into their constitution (women now represent over 50% of parliamentary seats).

Indirect is "moving away from/scared of/hiding from" a feared outcome, whereas Go Direct is moving "toward" the outcome you want. Go Direct is putting energy into having clarity on what you want so you can act with agency, rather than allowing events to unfold without your participation and then feeling resentful about the outcome.

Being proactive is 'going for it,' being the one who puts out the energy that will germinate into the outcome you want. Go Direct embodies the idea of "be the change you want to see in the world."

For the Long Term, not the Quick Hit:

Indirect strategies achieve a 'quick fix,' a momentary 'sugar high.'. But once on the sugar cycle, you need to keep getting the 'sugar fix'. Then you might need frequent reassurance or hold others' judgments at bay at every new meeting. You will micro-track and critique your performance (or the other person's behavior toward you in personal relationships). Indirect strategies effect an immediate but short term change in your state.

What you want is to have thoughts and take actions that build confidence for the long term, that truly build a life that gives you confidence. Go Direct is the 'protein diet' with which each thought gives you energy and sustenance for hours, each action contributes to an accomplishment that fuels your sense of satisfaction and trust in yourself.

You want to put your efforts into bigger picture wins that have a long tail halo, e.g., rather than doing a lot of little volunteer jobs seeking daily appreciation, put that time into a score on a visible strategic project that will be associated with your name going forward. Or work toward completing a speech or a book that will establish you as the 'go to' expert in your field. (And if daily volunteer jobs give you a sense of connectedness to other people, then do them for the right reason – to fulfill your sense of mission – but don't do them in order to get a compliment). In personal relationships, it's about not looking to the other person to validate you frequently, rather enjoy your life and who you are (which will magnetize them!)

Leaders Go Direct! A leader is only as good as how far out into the future you can have a vision. Regulating your internal confidence meter with attention on day to day interactions blinds you from creating a strategic vision. Not having a point of view, or making decisions for your own agenda and not the good of the group will interfere with your leadership. **And as a leader, you create the weather on your team**. I want you to see now that there's an energy associated with Indirect behaviors. It's mental and pressuring. Exhausting. Go Direct, in contrast, is energizing. It's a heart-based energy. It's about coming from your strengths, and seeing others'. Go Direct is about expanding your sense of contribution, and enjoying the ride.

Because you will put your efforts into initiatives that might take longer to see a result, you have to believe in yourself and trust your own judgment during the longer ramp-up time before launch. Yes, there is an element of risk to it that can tempt you toward seeking reassurance. For example, when I wrote my first book, I had to use my own judgment as to whether my ideas would be well-received, or whether only a few people would buy it and my entire effort would be a waste of time. On most of the days of writing, I got no feedback. Only occasionally I'd get input from my editor (who was a writer but didn't know anything about my field). I could only trust my own instincts, observe how my clients found the tools helpful, or crowdsource a book title (survey) to know if I was on the right track.

In fact, for that book, I interviewed literally the world's foremost experts and multiple NY Times bestselling authors such as David Allen on productivity, David Rock on leadership, Tony Schwartz on Performance, Dr. Sara Gottfried on women's hormones, pioneering neuroscientist Bruce McEwen and Dr. Joseph Michael Levry, founder of the fastest growing branch of yoga. I'd get off the phone and have a moment of: "WHO AM I to write this book??? On top of that I had someone in my inner circle who repeatedly said I wasn't showing good judgment with the book "distraction" – that it would sell only a few hundred copies and be a flop.

By trusting myself and staying objective about what worked vs where I was being overly critical (plus avoiding a tendency toward perfectionism), I finished writing the book. It was a worthy endeavor that has enabled me to impact thousands of people, be flown around the world as the 'go to' expert, and receive daily appreciation for the tools I provide. I would have still been 'just another coach and trainer' and not distinguished myself as an expert if I hadn't had the inner confidence to keep my eyes on a bigger prize, reassure *myself*, and stay objective about what would and wouldn't be valuable to the marketplace.

Win the Big Game, Not the Small Game:

When you Go Direct, your reward comes from the satisfaction of progress toward a worthy goal – helping a lot of people and a job well done. Because your contribution is usually more substantial or bigger in scope, the rewards are often more tangible as well – a bigger client, a meaningful project 'win', a salary raise, a hugely impactful charitable effort, a promotion, a business trip, an award.

When you Go Direct, you usually feel more in alignment with the empowered person you want to be. So, in that way, it gives you an immediate boost, but the reinforcement is more often internal than external. It 'feels right.' You are free from the usual frustration or exhaustion.

A key takeaway is that usually, when you Go Direct, you have bigger wins and get more recognition, but *without trying to get recognized*. This is similar to the idea of Win the Big Game, not the Small Game

For example, I coached a woman who worked in the equipment

leasing finance department of a large technology company. She was frustrated that her boss was not noticing and helping to promote her. She kept 'trying' to get recognized and supported. Using the strategies, you will learn about in Chapter 6, she instead focused on her purpose and the value she brings. There was a companywide breakdown in billing systems and everyone was frustrated. Passionate about resolving this major technology issue, she convened a productive monthly meeting of all parties interested in the matter. By the 3rd month, hers became the 'go to' meeting for company influencers. Because she was leading a process that started to get results and provided a valuable forum for 'get it done' types to make relationships, people were jockeying from across divisions to be invited.

She stopped her daily monitoring of whether her manager was validating her, or not. She focused attention away from her criticisms of him and poured herself into the visible win of finding an alternative to the company's broken technology issue. When she made progress there, she got extensive kudos. She made relationships that allowed her to have the influence she hoped she would have *through* her manager. She became a respected thought leader and then could write her own ticket. Just as important, she enjoyed her role again.

To paraphrase the popular MasterCard commercial, you can say: Indirect approaches to **get** her boss to make her feel valued: small game.

Making relationships with influencers across the company and solving a visible companywide problem: big game. (Priceless!)

Be Objective:

"I'm not good enough." Your self-doubt or self-criticism is not accurate; it's your view of yourself through your own filters. Go Direct means to see things as they are (or maybe a little more optimistically than they are), but not worse than they are. Accurate perception allows you to problem solve effectively.

For example, if you think you don't 'know enough' you might not go for the role or submit a proposal for the project. If your thinking is skewed by self-criticism, you might look at the one out of ten things you don't know and believe yourself unqualified, rather than thinking about the nine you do and how you could learn that tenth thing or pull in a resource to partner with.

Or you tell yourself "I'll never be a good public speaker." That's subjective. But when you break it down and look at it objectively, it's simply the case that you only need to learn to tell an attention-grabbing opening story. Or that your speaking is fine; you just need to learn how to ask for the business at the end. Or your content is great but your slides are too bogged down with words.

Remember that when a confidence concern gets activated, it will put you into a state of threat and skew your perspective. When you 'know in your mind' that you are great at what you do, but don't 'feel it in your bones,' you will be seeing through an emotional rather than a rational lens on the matter. All of us have "a part" of us that carries the feelings and burdens of feeling 'not enough' and when this part gets activated, it will hijack you and give you an out of control emotional response. It will set you up to interpret situations through your emotional lens ("I didn't get the role I wanted because I'm not good enough" or "because they are selfish jerks") instead of seeing the contextual clues in the situation that would help you understand ("they had to give the spot to the person from the company we merged with because that person knows the new product line better now" or "now that I think about it, the client who didn't hire me wasn't a good fit for the new services I offer", etc.). Sometimes your perspective about yourself is from the point of view of this younger self and needs to be updated to more objective views of your abilities. You want to learn the skill of taking the emotionality out of situations and staying fact-based. Objective!   (See Chapters 7, 8, 9, and page 140 to learn how)

Be Independent –

The idea of Go Direct is that it's possible for you to feel 'good in you' no matter what is going on around you. Even if your manager is limited and can't give you the support you need now. Even if an answer from that big fish prospect keeps getting postponed.   Even if your spouse is self-righteous and won't apologize. Or if the date you were hoping to have a chance with flakes out. Go Direct gives you the skillset to access that inner worthiness and self-trust anytime, anywhere, independent of how other people need to treat you.

Go Direct reminds you to seek autonomous ways of 'getting the goodies' in your life. Rather than needing to involve other people, you want to be able to feel satisfied from your contributions and the way you help people. Just as we need to breathe in air to take in (physical) oxygen, we are hardwired to need 'emotional oxygen.' It's the stuff that enables us to feel loved, worthy, valuable, deserving, attended to. You want relationships that provide reliable ways of getting this from loved ones, and when you have these nurturing relationships, you are usually able to call upon mental representations of that person's love even in moments you can't be in their presence.

Author Stephen Covey talks about progress from Dependent to Independent to Interdependent. Indirect strategies set up relationships where each partner is *dependent* on the other to act in a certain way so the other can get their needs met. Go Direct strategies enable you to have those healthy relationships in which two whole and *independent* people come together to complete each other's picture, not where the other person has to be your supply line to the emotional oxygen. Whether through work or extracurricular pursuits, you want to have autonomous ways of fulfilling your purpose, learning and growing, creative or athletic pursuits, meaningfully connecting with people, etc. You want ways of feeling centered and calm in your own body (whether through meditation or massage), so that on demand you can feel alive and at peace. (See Chapter 11 for strategies to do this)

Be Impeccable for your 50% -

This is the basis for being in your power: to "control what you can control" at any given moment. My book *Success under Stress* is based on the idea of Be Impeccable for your 50% - put your time and effort into becoming effective at what you CAN control before you ever allow yourself to focus on what you can't control. It's not about stress management; it's about self-management.

There's always things you can control, even in situations where it seems hopeless. For example, I coached a high potential woman at a large consumer products company. They had people on their team from all around the world in 3 time zones. Her boss was in Asia and she was in the US, and she started being left out of calls on a topic she thought she should 'own.' She took offense, and reacted. She was ready to 'call him out.' We discussed the many ways she could Be Impeccable for her 50%. This situation is a good example of where confidence and gender bias meet and it's helpful to be objective and tease them apart – because you would respond differentially.

She did her homework and became clear on her role and the way she could bring the most value. After this review, she decided that the project being discussed on the exclusionary call was not a priority for her so she let it go (though we did script a way she could ask her boss to be included if she ever found that the work on those team calls significantly overlapped with her objectives and merited her participation). Notice how, in this situation, being Objective enabled her to problem solve more effectively rather than calling up her manager with a complaint that might have been rightly or wrongly labeled as 'emotional.' If she truly was being excluded, then it would have been appropriate to ask for a seat at the table. In other words, it was more important to Be Impeccable for her 50% and do her part to make a good long-term relationship with her boss and peers.

To try on the idea of Go Direct, do this:

Whenever you are tempted to do an Indirect Behavior, I want you to do the following.

Step 1: Play out the scenario out in your imagination. What if you do your habitual Indirect behavior; what will happen next? How will the other person respond (or not respond)? What will you feel? Usually it will look something like: "I will try to control the other person and they will disappoint me" or "I will be frustrated with myself (or them) and lose focus." You might have the feeling of "there I go again!" or "this feels familiar, and it feels bad!"

Step 2: Check in with your gut how you feel about the speculated scenario.

Step 3: Imagine what it would be like to Go Direct. You trust yourself, you set boundaries, you keep your attention on what's real and what's important in the situation (you'll know how to do this better after you've read Chapters 5-11) and imagine how you'll feel *then*. My bet is that you'll feel empowered, and relieved. The comparison of how you imagine you'll feel based on scenario playing can help you make an intentional choice of how to behave in the situation.

Step 4: Go Direct! Reverse the curse and start to create a virtuous cycle.

The rest of this book provides you with solutions to shift from Indirect to Go Direct. You'll learn practical tools and mindset shifts you can carry out instantaneously inside of you. No one will ever know; they will only see a difference in how you act on the outside. These tools will enable you to show up as a calm, confident leader, to say "yes", to stay poised and above the fray, to take action and step into a more powerful version of yourself and your business. Without effortfully "trying", others will want to follow you. Others will want to be around your energy and have you lead projects and hire you as their provider. Welcome to the first day of the rest of your life...

POINTS TO REMEMBER

- Go Direct is the fast and lasting way to build confidence.
- Go Direct approaches are characterized by an approach that is Intentional, Proactive, Objective, Heart-based, and Self-trusting.
- Behaviors forge outcomes that are for the good of all, and win bigger results.
- Go Direct strategies enable you to get rewards and 'feel goods' through independent means so you don't need to involve others in your confidence regulating efforts.
- What you want is to shift from being a Confidence Seeker – someone who is trying to get confidence in the moment - to being a Confident Contributor – someone who acts from confidence when it counts.

NEXT STEPS

- Notice when you or others apply Go Direct strategies and how different it feels.
- Try the exercise in which you play out a scenario and compare your Indirect to Go Direct strategies. That will help you Go Direct in the moments that count. Share your experience and learn from other readers at **www.facebook.com/groups/confidencecounts**.
- If you 'know in your mind' you are really capable, but you don't 'feel it in your bones', there are 'quick fix' exercises I can help you with to root out your negative voice at it's source and gracefully feel that confidence at an emotional level. Learn more at **www.sharonmelnick.com/freedom**

Part II:

Your "Future"

Chapter 5:
From Instinctual to Intentional:
How to Act Confident when you Don't Feel
Confident

How many thoughts do you have a day to help you be confident? Neuroscientists have even estimated that as human beings we have about 60,000 thoughts during our waking hours each day.[3] Every one of these thoughts either takes you toward self-trust and makes a contribution to your confidence or takes you further away from it. Let's start with a temperature check, on average over the past week: what percentage of YOUR 60,000 thoughts a day are in the service of that unwavering confidence and focus on results, and what percentage takes you away from it?

How many of your 60,000 thoughts a day are helping you be confident,

and how many are taking you away from confidence?

I've asked thousands of people this question, and what do you think I usually hear? Answers span a range, but 50/50% or 70/30% are common responses (you are not alone!) I reply, "okay, 70 % of your thoughts direct you toward a confident contribution." And the audience members shake their head and say "No, the reverse." Most of my thoughts are away from a confident, results focus.

Take a moment and think about the opportunity for you. If we take a conservative number and say 70% of your thoughts are toward a confident, results focus and 30% are away from that each day. Even still, that's approximately 20,000 thoughts a day. If you multiply that by one week (7 days), that's 140,000 thoughts you are leaving on the table that could otherwise help you to be that confident contributor. (And that's just one person in your company, imagine multiplying that by all your colleagues too!)

So, you have 60,000 opportunities a day to make choices that will help you build and maintain your assuredness. That's a massive opportunity you've just unlocked! What's very organizing for your brain is to organize those 60,000 thoughts a day around a single intention, an intention of who you want to be.

The idea is that you can't always control the external results that you're going for. There are certain things that you can control and there are certain things that you can't (the biggest thing you CAN'T control is others' behavior). So, you want to focus on what is within your control. What's the best thing, really the only thing that you can control? That's right, who you show up as.

With the concept of Go Direct, we learned the importance of being able to generate confidence from within instead of involving others in that effort. We also reminded ourselves that you can't control other people's behavior, so you want to start being effective at controlling your own. As soon as you feel you must rely on your own resources, you might immediately feel stressed, prompting you to ask a question I often get: "How can I act confident when I'm not?"

In this chapter, you will learn a Do-It-Yourself (DIY) strategy so you can show up with unwavering confidence in your own abilities, regardless of the situation. You'll learn how to steer those 60,000 thoughts a day towards a confident outlook and presence. You'll know how to act as that secure and worthy person in the "lower right hand corner." This strategy is relevant for all confidence types.

Most of us go through our days trying to do the best we can with the mindset and tools available to us at that point in time. We react from our current level of confidence. But we are generally so overwhelmed we are just trying to get through the situation; we hope that others cooperate with our needs so we can advance the work and our business. But when we are resentful toward those who act from their own agendas and not ours, we regret the way we react and often obsess about it. When faced with a difficult person, we struggle to rise above it or get unstuck from it.

In this chapter, you will learn to shift from reactive to intentional. Instead of putting your efforts into controlling the response you want to get from other people, you decide who YOU want to be . . . and then think, feel, and act in the service of that person. Similarly, you are often focused on the external results you are trying to achieve. But if others don't call you back, don't send the email you asked, don't sign the contract, act dismissive, etc., it derails you. You feel frustrated. You feel under pressure to prove yourself or achieve business results, but then you feel out of control of achieving those results. It might make you doubt your own abilities or live in fear of consequences.

To be intentional is to first have a picture of the kind of outcome you want to create. When you have clear intention, it orients your thoughts towards the aspects of the situation you can control as opposed to those that you can't.

An important step to achieving any goal is to become the 'YOU' that can think, feel, and act in accordance with reaching that goal. I call this version of you your **"Horizon Point."** This is taken from the visual that you are the captain of your own ship. A captain's job is to fix her sights on the destination and keep steering the boat with moment-to-moment course corrections towards that point. Out on the high seas, there will be stormy waves, icebergs, and other ships to steer clear of. The captain can't control the stormy waters, but the captain can control herself to stay steady, focused, and agile to steer the ship through them.

Similarly, it is easy to get sucked into the vortex of others' expectations and daily demands. The idea of your Horizon Point is to impose a sense of purpose and control upon your day – i.e., my purpose is to display the qualities and attributes of who I need to be in order to be successful – so that you don't hope you show up confident but then default into merely reacting to others' behavior. No matter what challenge you face, you can always control who you are in response to it.

Your Horizon Point serves both as an internal guidance system and as a filter. In terms of an internal guidance system, there is a bundle of fibers in your brain called the reticular activating system (RAS)[4] that is in part responsible for sorting out information you want to focus on and the information that you don't. A clear intention allows your RAS to filter in stimuli that fulfill that intention and filter out what doesn't. Once you have defined who you want and need to be, you can go through your day being **intentional.**

Each moment, each interaction, each meeting – you have a choice to either act consciously and proactively in the service of creating that internal experience, or, conversely, not be intentional and let the experience happen to you. As you are about to take an action, you might even want to ask yourself "Is this action going to help me be at my Horizon Point, or not?"

To translate this into practical steps – try this approach. As you go through your day, instead of focusing only on the tasks or appointments you need to fulfill, bring more of your focus inward. It's your internal experience that sets your level of confidence – or stress. Focus on that internal experience of who you need to be at your Horizon Point. This shift in focus will ensure that despite moment-to-moment ups and downs, you're always progressing towards the result you desire. By maintaining the mindset of the person you need to be in order to be successful, you maximize the chance you will actually achieve that success.

It's important to do this exercise because the rest of the strategies in this book will help you show up as this confident, bold, inner-trusting woman – no matter what's going on around you.

Finding Your Horizon Point: Exercise 1

How do you figure out who you want to be at your Horizon Point? Start by listing the qualities, attributes and skills of who YOU WANT TO BE. You should also identify qualities, attributes and skills that your organization requires of you, or who you would need to be in your own business in order to be successful. Your Horizon Point should be the overlap between what you want for yourself and what your work requires of you.

Try to list qualities and attributes and behaviors you do want for yourself, not those you don't want. It may be the case that you don't know what your bigger picture goals are for yourself and that's ok. Whether you are happy in your current work or life circumstances or not, your Horizon Point is less about the external goals you want to achieve for yourself (e.g., next level promotion, an income level, a fitness goal) and more about who do you need to be as a person in order to make that outcome happen. Notice how your Horizon Point is all about what is within your control.

I want you to think about the qualities and attributes of who you need to be. Think about the results you will forge and the experience you will have of yourself when you're consistently showing up with those qualities and attributes (Watch out, world!). You could also allow yourself a moment imagining how other people will respond to you when you consistently act like that person. You don't want to act at your Horizon Point in order to make a specific perception, but this illustrates one of the tenets of Go Direct; you often get the recognition and cool opportunities but without trying to get them!

You want your Horizon Point to be your new filter. Ask yourself as you go through your day, "Am I acting in the service of my Horizon Point? What would it look like to show up as my Horizon Point in this situation? What tools did I learn from Sharon to help me be at my Horizon Point now?"

To help illustrate this, here is how Nikki, Linda, and Sonya identified their Horizon Points.

Nikki's Horizon Point – Perfectionist/Criticizer

- Be calm and steady.
- Support other people to problem solve – coach people more instead of being harsh with them
- Beat herself up less.
- Connecting and collaborate more than control people.
- Lift up from execution, Stay a strategic thinker.

Linda's Horizon Point - Performer

- Be acknowledged and valued by her manager.
- Be Respected. *
- Have a seat at the table.
- Be Confident, not so hard on herself, take things less seriously.
- Delegate more effectively.

*I am calling attention here to the fact that Linda wants to be acknowledged and respected by her manager. This is an outcome that is not within her control, though the best way to influence it is by who she shows up as. She can't control being respected, but she can control being worthy of Respect. Or Respecting Herself. These attributes would be more appropriate as part of her Horizon Point and would guide her to know how to act.

Sonya's Horizon Point - Protector

- Be fearless.

- Stay focused.

- Own her value – feel worthy of charging more for her work.

- Become a go-to expert in her field.

- Put herself out more.

- Take action as soon as she has ideas instead of procrastinating.

Now you try the exercise. The more specific you are about exactly what qualities and skills describe who you need to be, the more likely you will be able to remember to be that person in the moment. The ship's captain doesn't take out the map to start figuring out where she wants to go after the 20-foot waves hit. The captain has a clear destination ahead of time. The clearer you are upfront, the easier it is to check in with yourself and know whether you are or are not on course towards being that person.

What are the qualities and attributes you want to have at YOUR Horizon Point? (Download the audio training in which I walk you through the steps to discover YOUR Horizon Point at www.sharonmelnick.com/horizonpoint)

_____

_____

_____

<u>Finding Your Horizon Point: Exercise 2:</u>

If you took the first exercise seriously, you probably have a minimum of 5 or 10 qualities and attributes listed that cover a spectrum of things you need in order to effectively achieve results. In order to make this easy to refer to in the moment, you need a way of encapsulating the essence of that list. An effective way to do this is to relate your Horizon Point to a concise phrase, an image, or a tangible feeling in your body.

To help motivate you, here are a few more examples of how my clients cut through complexity and challenges to reach their goals fast by setting an intention to think, feel, and act like the ideal they set as their Horizon Points:

Pamela's Horizon Point (Pamela was a Performer and Protector)

Pamela was a junior partner at a big 4 consulting firm. Her common indirect behavior was to respond immediately to incoming emails with long technical replies (to get other people to think she was responsive). She took on a long list of tedious administrative matters. She worried about how others judged her. What she really wanted at her Horizon Point was to become a senior leader. Was she acting in the service of that Horizon Point each day? No! Here is a glimpse of who she wanted to be at her Horizon Point:

- Know her value, and share insights more with C-suite clients.
- Enjoy thinking strategically.
- Be a great mentor and coach to the people on her team.
- Not stress about what other people think of her.
- Have time to start training for a marathon.

She decided on **"Confident Leader"** to encapsulate her Horizon Point. And then she started to think and act like one! She inserted time into her day to prepare strategic advice for her C-suite meetings. She started to mentor her team members to take over the email monitoring functions, and she became more intentional about how she spent her own time to allow for running training outside of work. She asked for assignments that gave her more exposure to senior leaders. Six months later, she was promoted to the head of the regional office. Nine months later, she was placed on international decision-making committees for the firm. That summer she ran her first marathon. The concept of the Horizon Point may sound fluffy but see how powerful the results can be!

Ginnie's Horizon Point (Ginnie's type was "Confident Leader")

Ginnie is responsible for the supply chain at an international fashion company. Her organization was changing the supply from A to Z, lots of change! In her fast-paced fashion company where both the creative designers and the marketing rock stars were drama queens, reactivity was common. Here's a sample of who she wanted to be at her Horizon Point:

- Rational, not reactive
- Above the fray – positive collaborator
- Sought after calm, steady role model for embracing change

Her encapsulating phrase was **"Poised Change Agent."** This became her filter as she went throughout her day: "How can I show up as a Poised Change Agent? What did I learn from my coach Sharon to stay poised? How can I be intentional and influence change in this situation?" Within 3 months of Ginnie's showing up as a Poised Change Agent, her CEO noticed that she was a leader, even on the senior management team "She's a role model. The kind of person that I want to be leading our teams." Then she was promoted into a global role.

Pat's Horizon Point (Pat was a Confident Leader with Performer as secondary type)

Pat was in my "C-school" program, and worked in a male-dominated environment where she had to deal with unsubstantiated critical performance feedback. Her Horizon Point came in particularly handy when she had to walk into a performance feedback meeting she expected would be uncomfortable. As she said:

At my Horizon Point, I am "Pat at the Podium" – calm, open, composed, a reminder of all the times in which I was a well-received speaker in front of the room. I walked in to my performance assessment as "Pat at the Podium" with a manager who is insecure and unsupportive. It enabled me to disarm everything she said. Instead of crumbling, I was able to say things like: This is important information for me to have, I am open to hearing your input. I asked really good questions (as any speaker in front of the room would ask in order to reply appropriately). I asked for examples and more information, even though the manager couldn't supply any. She got frustrated with my composure. I came out feeling great and knowing exactly what my next steps were. It's so tangible that I feel I really am her. She is always there with me; she's a fundamental part of who I am. Even though she gets lost at times, I can call her up and know that 'I got this'!

Dionne's Horizon Point (Dionne was a coach who was a Performer)

Dionne is a coach who wanted to differentiate herself from all the other coaches so she could be seen as the go-to expert and grow her business. As is the case for most business owners, she was afraid to choose a specific niche, out of concern it would cut off potential business. Plus, she wanted to be bold but had a persona as a 'nice girl' and didn't want a niche that would be too provocative or radical.

What she wanted at her Horizon Point was to:

- Know my value.
- Take action as soon as I have ideas, not procrastinate.
- Position myself powerfully in a niche.

- Be a champion for women executives.

Her Horizon Point was "**Fearless and Focused**." As she would go through her day reminding herself to be Fearless and Focused, she started to take consistent action. (She even ended up writing a book called *Give Fear the Finger*; I call that fearless!) She positioned herself deeper into the niche of being a champion for senior women executives. What were the results? Month after month, highest income ever! And she published her popular e-book and attained regular speaking engagements, even being flown to Europe to speak.

Jeanine's Horizon Point (Jeanine was a Perfectionist/Criticizer)

Jeanine was the head of production at a fashion company. She had a short fuse. When her direct reports lined up outside her door all day to ask her questions, she would snap at them and be intolerant of their mistakes. She didn't sleep well at night and she experienced high turnover on her team. Instead, she wanted to maintain her high standards but be an effective coach/mentor to her team members, exude more calm, and sleep at night.

She changed her perspective and made her encapsulating phrase, "I'm the **Chief Problem-Solving Officer**." From that point on, when her staff would come to her with question or mistakes, she would welcome them because she viewed her role as the one to help them solve their problems. Turnover on her team was reduced and profits were the highest in the company's history for 6 months straight. She rode a high for a few years and then decided to start her own company and, of course, was successful right off the bat because of her marriage between results and relationships.

Karen's Horizon Point (Karen was a Performer and Perfectionist/Criticizer)

For her Horizon Point, Stacy wanted to stay at the **"Top of the Mountain**." It was a visual that reminded her of times she had been at the top of the mountain on vacation. For her, it represented the idea that she could see all the things going on in the valley yet not have to be involved in the details, or do it all herself. Whenever she would call up that image throughout the day, it would remind her to lift her sights and, instead of reacting automatically to the workflow, keep her eyes on the bigger, strategic goals that she wants to achieve. This was important to her because she joined my Confident Influential Leader program in order to get to her next level.

By being more confident, she was able to assert herself in meetings with senior management. By being caring but firm, she was finally able to take action with an underperforming direct report who we discovered was the primary cause of her having to micromanage at such a detailed level, given the level of risk involved in the project. Then she could delegate more of her tasks. With some of the time that was freed up, she thought about the best way for her small organization to be configured, and then proposed a re-organization plan to her busy boss. Her boss approved the plan and she was immediately promoted to be the senior strategic head of the whole group.

Carol's Horizon Point (Carol was highly successful Perfectionist/Criticizer and Performer)

Carol sells insurance and works in a small group financial firm. She is Type A and a hard worker. She is critical of herself and has low tolerance for other people who aren't up to her standards. She was recently referred a client from a lawyer and the first thing she said to herself was "You better not screw this up!" What she wanted was to go through her days of back-to-back appointments but get a better return on her investment of time and feel more in a flow rather than so pressured. Specifically, she wanted:

- Grow her business by getting more clients.

- Be poised and not so anxious.

- Have more balance/time with children.

- Be confident and less self-critical.

Initially, her Horizon Point was **"Million Dollar Producer"** and that would have been a perfectly apt one for her. But what she really aspired to was to grow her business but be less hard-charging so instead, she focused her encapsulating phrase on that outcome, **"Effortless Flow."** (I included this one because I thought you might want to license it from Carol royalty free!) She would ask herself "How could I approach this situation with more flow? How could I accomplish this with less effort?" By being more intentional about her business practices and streamlining her efforts (e.g., convening a monthly networking event for referral sources rather than running around having 1:1 meetings all month), she was able to put an extra 50k in her pocket in 6 months while spending two afternoons a week with her children. She delegates what's not in her sweet spot to her staff, and she is saying yes to bigger opportunities that have grown her business.

The concept of the Horizon Point sounds fluffy, but can you see how powerfully it works?!!!

Take another look at your list of qualities and attributes and behaviors. Is there an image that comes to mind, or a phrase? Be creative and have fun with it. Try to make the essence of your Horizon Point something that is inspiring and motivating for you. Spend a little time on this (and don't worry; it can always evolve over time) because all of the other strategies in this book are intended to help you be THAT person in the moments it counts. Make the purpose of each work day to act in accordance with your Horizon Point. Especially in the midst of situations that could derail you or set you up to act counterproductively, remember who you have defined that you want to be. How would "insert your **Encapsulating Phrase** here" handle this situation?

What is your encapsulating phrase for your Horizon Point?

(Download the audio training in which I walk you through the steps to discover YOUR Horizon Point at

www.sharonmelnick.com/horizonpoint)

Keep your phrase and image front-and-center in your attention with reminder pictures, post-it notes or screen savers, and by repeating your statement throughout the day. Allow yourself to get a little lift as you visualize or have the feeling in your body of you rocking your world! Anticipate situations in which you might be reactive or get deflated or overwhelmed and build your response before you get into these moments. Script out and mentally rehearse how you will act in the service of your Horizon Point next time.

Your Horizon Point helps you act with intention. It helps you show up as who YOU want to be. It's the answer to the question: "How can I show up confident when I don't feel confident?" You don't have to feel confident yet in order to have the intention to show up as your Horizon Point. Have the intention first. Direct your attention toward it. Keep turning the pages of this book (or join the Confident Leader coaching program) to learn the skills to support your intention.

How can I act at my Horizon Point on demand when I'm in a difficult moment?

Try this exercise…

Become who you are at your Horizon Point in this very moment. That's right, embody that person you want to be. Go ahead and try it..

Notice…what did you "do" to upload being that person? Did you change your posture? Breathe differently? Did you imagine a visual of you being that person?

Now go back and become who you are at your Horizon Point again. Notice what you did this time. Did you think of the memory of a time you felt like that person and try to recreate it? Did you imagine a future version of yourself being that way? Did you tell yourself something?

Note ALL the sensory access strategies you used to become your Horizon Point. You can call upon these strategies anytime, anywhere to become your Horizon Point on demand.

(I have a popular audio training that shows you step-by-step how to change your 60,000 thoughts a day from doubting, stressed, or distracted to "in the service of your Horizon Point." Using a fun metaphor, it shows you how to be the DJ of your own mental iPod. Go now to **www.sharonmelnick.com/DJ** to download it so you can practice making each of your 60,000 thoughts a day in the service of your Horizon Point)

In summary, acting at your Horizon Point helps you rise above the confidence crunch and reactivity of the moment, and puts you in charge of how you show up. It can help you create quick and tangible wins for yourself and others. When you are on the vicious cycle caused by Indirect Path behaviors, you are usually just trying to get through the moment. But **when you act towards your Horizon Point, you uplift yourself out of the moment and act towards a 'better' long term version of yourself (or continue with the current best aspects with yourself.)** Your Horizon Point generally inspires you to be personally effective AND to make a contribution to other people. You can see from the above stories that it ejected people from their everyday challenges and facilitated their instant confidence.

No matter what stresses are going on outside of you, you can always control how you think, feel, and act — and by doing so, you can always create the experience you want to have of yourself. Ultimately, your ability to create the success you want is determined by this internal experience you create.

POINTS TO REMEMBER

- Organize your 60,000 thoughts a day in the service of a single intention to show up confident

- Your "Horizon Point" is a "Do it Yourself" strategy. A reminder of what you can control, namely 'who you want and need to be' in order to achieve desired external results.

- Define your Horizon Point in two parts: 1. What are the qualities and attributes of who you want to be? 2. Find a phrase that captures the essence of it so you can remember it.

- Make it your purpose and filter to act at your Horizon Point throughout the day.

- You can embody who you want to be at your Horizon Point on demand.

NEXT STEPS

- Allow me to walk you through the exercise so You can discover YOUR Horizon Point, go to **www.sharonmelnick.com/horizonpoint. Plus** there I provide resources how you can create a visual that reminds you of your Horizon Point everyday and in every meeting!

- Download the audio training how to make your 60k thoughts/day toward your Horizon Point **www.sharonmelnick.com/DJ.**

- Come up with a Horizon Point that jazzes you so you can use the rest of the book to know how to show up as that person! Share your Horizon Point with me and other readers so we can give you some love around it at **www.facebook.com/groups/confidencecounts**

Chapter 6:
From Worried to "Worthy":
How to Speak Up and Take Risks When You Are Afraid of Being Judged

"There are going to be people along the way who will try to undercut your success or take credit for your accomplishments or your fame. But if you just focus on the work and you don't let those people sidetrack you, someday when you get where you're going, you'll look around and you will know that it was you and the people who love you who put you there. And that will be the greatest feeling in the world.

-Taylor Swift upon accepting the Grammy award for her album "1989"

In this chapter, you will learn how to 'cut out that middleman' and instead Go Direct. You will learn to Rise Above your own judgments of yourself, and instead put your energies directly toward the contribution you want to make. This chapter will be especially relevant to you if you are a Protector or someone who hesitates to speak up, go for it, take a risk, etc.

Let's start with a typical example: You are in a meeting and you have something valuable to say. You want to speak up but then you start having that inner debate: "Should I say it, or not? Will others think I am smart or is my comment mundane? Does everyone else know this already? Will they lose respect for me? If I say this, will they still hire me? They haven't heard me in the past; will I be wasting my breath?"

(As you go through this chapter, you might want to call to mind a specific situation in which you you've held yourself back from speaking up, taking a risk, raising your hand, asking for full fee, negotiating for resources, standing your ground, etc.)

What do you say to yourself that has convinced you in the past to not speak up or go for it? (e.g., "I'm not ready", "I'm not as smart as them", "What will the political fallout be?")

Write what you say to yourself here:

_____

What you just wrote is the doubt or self-criticism that appeared in the left-hand corner of our triangle diagram

This negative conviction about yourself sets you up to do an Indirect path behavior. You will hesitate, hide, or keep expectations low so as not to disappoint or get criticized.

That's the old way, Indirect. Here's the new way, Go Direct!

The skill you want to develop is to shift your focus off you and onto the contribution you can make. You do this by taking yourself out of it, i.e., "It's not about you, honey!" Instead, focus on your purpose. How can you focus on your purpose when you are afraid of making a mistake or how others will judge you? Here are 5 strategies to do that:

Strategy #1: Focus on your End User

When you have an imagined movie in your head of people judging you, you've just triggered performance anxiety. No wonder you're nervous! Your perspective is one of others' eyes on you. In the blink of an eye, you can switch your perspective. Instead, focus on looking outward and giving to your End User.

Who is your End User?

That is the person (or people) who will benefit from your speaking up, asking for resources, offering ideas, having more responsibility. This is the person(s) you will help, or who will have their life improved if you take a more confident action.

Be so filled with a sense of purpose that all you can think about is how to bring more value to your End User.

For example, last month, I spoke at the Healthcare Businesswomen's conference for women leaders – there were 900 women in the audience. It was the first time I told the "Tipper Gore White House invite" story on stage. I could have felt deathly nervous – as most women (and men) do when speaking in front of a large room. But I was so filled with my sense of purpose to catalyze confidence in the aspirant audience members that I had no bandwidth for their potential judgment of me.

How did I do it? As I prepared and as I walked on the stage, I strategized about what action I want people to take when they leave my presentation. Then I do what is pictured in the Microsoft television commercials. Ever seen them? A child is featured in front of a chalkboard with a schematic drawing above her head indicating she dreams of being an astronaut someday. I do the same thing. I picture the outcome I want for you as the audience member. I imagine you as a Confident Contributor. Then I reverse engineer my talk so you will have the beliefs, the inspiration, and the tools to act boldly when we finish our time together. I'm so intent on helping you have that outcome that I pour myself into the effort. Hundreds of women came up to me afterwards, saying they "loved my energy" and how much they 'resonated' with what I said – I think that was their way of saying they felt I was present, and that they had gained the intended takeaways that would help them take action. (Notice the feedback about 'positive energy' you'll get when you too Go Direct)

Let's go back to an example where you are not speaking up or holding yourself back.

In the situation you identified, start by identifying your End User.

Who is your end user?

• If you are in a meeting to discuss a new policy, your End User could be your customers or if you are in HR or IT, it could be your internal employees. What's a better decision that could be made with the information that you might share?

• If you are making a presentation to propose new ideas or changes to the business, your End User might be other functional groups in your company.

• If you are writing a memo, your End User might simply be your manager and team members who will make use of the data or ideas in your memo.

• If you are writing marketing materials for your business or wanting to get on video, your End User might be people who suffer from a problem you can help or referral sources.

• In personal situations, the people who might be helped by your speaking up, negotiating, or asking for resources might be your children, spouse or community members.

• When giving a speech, the End Users are your audience members.

• If you are planning an event the End Users are the attendees who experience your efficiency or the beauty of the set up.

• When you think about your End User in the context of taking on more responsibility, think of all the people in your group or department (or your customers) who will be helped when you bring your smart and collaborative leadership to the role.

• If you are considering taking a risk to grow your business, think of how you can help more people if you scale.

• In your relationship, think of how what you say will benefit the quality of your relationship (how it could raise the bar of safety, communication, and respect between you)

- If it's setting boundaries, think of how you being freed up and strong will benefit other people in your life (as well as yourself).

Anytime you're in a situation where you're having that inner debate, "Should I speak up? Should I go for it?" I want you to take yourself out of it. It's not about you! It doesn't really matter really whether *you* think you're good enough. All that matters is that you are able to be helpful and bring value to other people. Let your passion to help your End User help you rise above your doubt and go for it.

Strategy #2: Be the champion and steward of your beneficiaries.

I'm going to wager a bet that you are going to be EXCELLENT at this strategy. How do I know that? Because this is a strategy based on love, and I imagine that comes naturally to you. In a study of cadets at West Point (the U.S. military leader training academy), what do you think was the #1 trait of the most successful leaders? The capacity to love![iii] They made decisions based on the needs of their charges. They were willing to get outside of themselves for their people. Leaders saw themselves as the champions and stewards of their end users.

Many of you want to have a big impact and help a lot of people with your talents or your craft. I run a program that helps talented business owners become the go-to experts in their fields. One of the 'on fire' women in this program is a divorce lawyer who wants to help more people. She's a lawyer who re-trained in a more modern approach called Collaborative Divorce (helps divorcing couples come to a mutually agreed upon, negotiated settlement without the threat of court. It offers a civilized, solutions-based approach to ending a relationship).

Whenever she was tempted to think "Who am I to write a book" or "Who am I to give a TED talk" or "I don't have time to do that," I encouraged her to see herself as the champion and steward of her potential end users (all the people unhappily married or about to get divorce). She was able to get started on her book and speech as she began to take on the mindset: "Not on my watch will people suffer. As long as I know something about how people can amicably separate from a marriage without ruinous emotional and financial pain, I'm not going to let my daily life interfere with getting my message out…"

If loving comes easily to you, then use it as a strength. In those situations where you're having the inner debate, pour yourself into the beneficiary of your taking confident action. Let that give you the courage to speak up and go for it.

Strategy #3: Courage is love.

If you are considering speaking up with an unpopular message, you will need courage. As the great Chinese philosopher Lao Tzu once said: "From caring comes courage."

Here are three case studies where women spoke up, persevered, and took a risk to act with courage, and you can too!

Mia brought me to do the Confident Leader training at her company. Here's how she used the skills she learned to navigate a tough situation that would have caused her to leave the company had she not succeeded: Her company just finished a restructuring and she was assigned to work with a boss with whom she had worked previously. Problem was, she had a terrible experience with him in the past. He was a micromanager, negative, and dismissive. Everything was on the line for her and she had to decide: leave the company or do something to forge a better working relationship with him. Here is the email I received from her a few weeks after my training to her team:

"I had an extremely good but intense talk with my new boss. My heart was beating when I walked in, I was totally scared. It was a major risk because I had to be honest and stay factual, not emotional. I kept repeating the mantra 'courage is love'.

The way you coached us to open the discussion worked like magic, as he immediately understood "What's in it for him" if he does not work with me to help improve the organization.

He was extremely open and listened. I don't think anyone had been so honest with him before. He asked for examples and admitted he had done the things I reported. He asked me to continue on-going feedback and committed to change. He agreed to the team structure I proposed! I realized only after our meeting that I was the one setting the standard and holding him to it – and that I will be "coaching" him! It is really strange but good. It totally freed me up!

Honestly, if he had not been open to my feedback, I would have left the company that day.

I would not have managed this crisis without your recent training here; I am forever grateful. This is only the start of the journey, but it feels so wonderful to already be acting at my Horizon Point!"

Following the idea of focusing on your end user, think about who will be helped, or protected, or served by your input? Rather than questioning yourself, be proud of your integrity. Women are often willing to negotiate harder or take courageous action when they do so on behalf of others (it also helps to circumvent bias against women who can be perceived as aggressive when negotiating on their own behalf). See yourself a champion for the truth. Allow that to help you persevere against odds.

A woman in my Confident Influential Leader coaching program worked at a technology company. She was in a role she no longer enjoyed and wanted to transition into a diversity role. On her own time, she had already engaged in activities that helped show her leadership in diversity-related issues. She said it was hard for her to ask her manager to do this: "I am almost embarrassed taking a stand; I have a hard time tooting my own horn." So, she had made only timid requests, or dropped hints at what she wanted. When she approached other women and they gave blank stares, or questioned why she was "shaking things up," she sometimes got discouraged.

This idea that "courage is love" helped her step up her efforts. She no longer saw her transition as only about "what I want for me in terms of salary, commute" (which wasn't very compelling for the company and they had refused her office swap request 2 times before). She took herself out of it and now pictured her transition in terms of all the diverse talent she could help. Hers was a company with an old-school culture of hierarchy and lack of diversity. She re-ignited her passion, thinking about the benefit starting a women's leadership network could bring – how they could help drive the culture to improve customer satisfaction and the engagement of their diverse talent. Once she felt in her body that she was the steward of the company's culture, she wrote up a strategy plan for diversity initiatives. Her boss's boss couldn't help but see the value she was bringing, even before they had created a role for her, and then she was given the new role as an inevitability.

Can you focus on your end user to speak up with an unpopular opinion and risk everything? Joy did. She is a senior leader in Human Resources and had a moment in which she had to act with courage. At a town hall with the company's senior leaders, the company CEO said something that was demeaning toward women (In 2014, it was a comment to the effect that women should be home baking cookies.) He was not aware of his blunder and certainly not of it's effect on the senior women leaders in the room. Joy had to think through how to respond.

She decided to show courage. She came home and only half-jokingly told her husband that she might get fired the next day, asking if 'it would be ok'. The next day she took a deep breath and walked into the room to have an honest talk with the CEO. She was fortified by the idea of protecting the culture of the company, as well as the liability of having a CEO who was clueless to a major demographic trend. She explained the lack of awareness he had displayed. She coached him with language to say to his management team, along the lines of "apologies, and help me to learn." She put forth her best pitch and was honest with him, but he refused to do so. Well, at least that's what he said to her face. But at the next opportunity, he followed her script and it was well-received! I witnessed her have this same courage when we provided feedback together to a client I coached at her company. Joy was direct but pleasant, focusing on the positive path forward - and the feedback was well received. You can feel from my description that Joy definitely has the energy of a Confident Leader!

Is your hesitation to speak up Fear or Frustration?

Have a nuanced understanding of the reason behind your hesitation to speak up with confidence. Diagnose whether your hesitation has to do with your own self-doubt (Fear) and/or with the knowledge that you've spoken up too many times before and not been heard or had your ideas acted on (Frustration). Pinpoint what phrase you are telling yourself that "blocks" you from speaking up. Is it: "My ideas are not smart" or "I'm not ready" or "I am afraid of being judged?" If so, your block comes from fear and self-doubt – i.e., it's a Confidence issue - and you want to use the exercises in this chapter to rise above fear and speak up.

Is your negative self-talk more about the response you'll get based on experience (e.g., along the lines of "They never listen anyway I might as well save my breath.") Then it's more due to frustration and it could be due to either your influencing approach, to gender bias, or both. See Chapter 13 for elaboration.

Strategy #4: See yourself as an equal.

The idea here is: don't make it hard to speak up because you make the other person 'bigger and better' than you.   Many of us can be confident in situations where we perceive we are on a level playing field with others but immediately deflate our confidence tires when we judge others as being more than we are.

For example, I have a colleague who started an amazing program to help women entrepreneurs get capital to grow their business. She was telling me about an upcoming phone conference with a woman she was going to ask to be a sponsor and Honorary Chair of her initiative – she was nervous! As she described to me, this woman was a BIG DEAL. "She is the CEO of a company, she partners with an Oscar-winning actor on his foundation, etc." Which led my friend to question: "Why would she want to sponsor US?"

My colleague was also concerned about how she would establish her credibility given that she had an MBA, worked at elite institutions but tried to get funding herself and couldn't (which is why she wanted to start this initiative) – i.e., how could she purport to teach others?

Here's what you want to immediately notice. First, my friend put this CEO woman "1 up" and herself "1 down". Second, she was caught up in her head with her own ideas about what would make her credible in the potential sponsor's eyes, but wasn't thinking about it from the potential sponsor's point of view.

So, I helped her apply the idea of Focus on your End User.

The first step was to take herself out of it and not keep worrying about how SHE would be evaluated. I encouraged her to reframe where her credibility would come from. Not from having started your own company and having difficulty getting funded – rather, it comes from knowing the pain of millions of women with a helpful business who can't get funded. What gives her credibility in this situation is the empathy she has for the beneficiaries of the women's funding initiative. If the sponsor is going to sign on, it's because she shares a mission to help the end users, not whether my friend got funded or not in her past.

Her credibility comes from her ability to describe the situation of these potential beneficiaries in such a way that it is compelling to the funder – whether that means using data to help her evaluate the size of the problem or having her heartstrings tugged at the tragedy of the women or tying the upside potential of the initiative to the vision of the funder. The conversion point will come when she connected the initiative to the funder's desired legacy.

Remember, take yourself out of it; it's not about you. You are not doing it for you; you are doing it to bring value to your end users.

Strategy #5: "Play to Win!"

Just do a gut check and see if your behaviors have set you up in life to "Play not to Lose". This approach leads to enormous frustration because you put out a lot of energy but never feel like you arrive at the outcome. If this resonates for you, think about the success you *truly* want. Think about the difference you truly want to make and all the people you want to impact. And in your heart of hearts how much you really want the next level salary/income or title or 'say' in how things go in your organization. Feel deserving of it and... Play to Win!

Strategy #6: Worry about the right things.

Are you a worrier? Are you a person whose mind is always going, "What if I say this? What are they going to think about it?" Not a problem, hope is not lost! I'm not going to take your worrying from you; we're just going to channel it effectively!

If you need to worry, then worry about the needs of your end user. Try to describe their concerns, their challenges, and their opportunities even better than you've described them now, which of course will help you be successful with them. Because the more you can describe their problems, challenges, and opportunities to them better than they can describe them to themselves, the more you will be seen as that trusted advisor, and the more you're implicitly seen has having the solution. So, pour your worrying energy into describing the challenges, the benefits, and solutions that you're going to bringing to your end user.

In sum, take yourself out of it and pour yourself into your purpose. Use your focus on your end user to rise above and act at your Horizon Point in the moments when it counts.

As Anais Nin once famously inspired us to remember: "Life shrinks or expands in proportion to one's courage."

POINTS TO REMEMBER

- Shift your focus off of you and onto the contribution you want to make. Take yourself out of it!
- Act to benefit your 'End User', those helped by your confident action
- Use your capacity to love to have courage and act as a steward of your 'End Users'
- See yourself as an equal rather than judge yourself '1 down' from others
- Stop playing not to lose, Play to Win!
- Are you a worrier? Channel your worry into understanding the needs of your end user.

NEXT STEPS

- Facing a situation where it's important that you speak up or take a risk in your life? If you want to jump in and get my help, contact me at **sharon@sharonmelnick.com**. Or check out "C-school" (**www.sharonmelnick.com/cwc**) or the Confident Influential Leader virtual coaching program **www.sharonmelnick.com/cil** that has helped hundreds of other people like you 'feel ready' and speak up so they could expand their role or get promoted.

Chapter 7:
From Self-Critical to Self-Confident:
How to Change your Inner Voice to Know you are "Good Enough"

"Even our worst enemies don't talk about us the way we talk to ourselves." One of my favorite role models Arianna Huffington calls this voice "the obnoxious roommate living in our head. It feeds on putting us down and strengthening our insecurities and doubts. I wish someone would invent a tape recorder that we could attach to our brains to record everything we tell ourselves. We would realize how important it is to stop this negative self-talk. It means pushing back against our obnoxious roommate with a dose of wisdom. I have spent many years trying to evict my obnoxious roommate and have now managed to relegate her to only occasional guest appearances in my head."

In this chapter, you are going to learn to become the landlord of your own mental real estate. We are going to follow Arianna's guidance to push back using wisdom and humor. And we're going to have a civilized discussion with your "obnoxious roommate" in which YOU will prevail – she will agree to leave without drama, and validate that you are in charge. Now there's a negotiation you actually might WANT to enter!

This chapter is relevant for all Confidence Types, and will be particularly helpful to the Perfectionist/Criticizer, Protector, and Confident Leader.

What's the skill you'll build? To shift from **Subjective to Objective**. Subjective is the way you think about yourself through your own filters. When you think that you're 'not enough' (not smart enough, not thin enough, etc.), when you feel 'one down' compared to others, or when you think you did 'a bad job'...all of these are subjective. This is your opinion and your perspective, it's not fact. Objective is about the facts, what's true, what can be empirically measured and benchmarked.

For example, I recently attended a worthwhile gathering of leaders at the United Nations for International Women's Day. On a break, I spoke with the moderator of the just-finished panel.

She was in a responsible position developing programs for women around the world. In my mind, I was thinking how talented she was that she had impacted so many women and how inspiring it was she was interested in incorporating my ideas into their programs (Brief digression: I said "yes" this time ;-)

As the organizer of the event walked by, the moderator woman called out to her and said, "I'm sorry I didn't do a good job, I wanted to do a wrap-up summary at the end of the panel". I furrowed my brow and did a double-take. What?? I took a lot of notes and found her to be a very structuring moderator. It would never have even occurred to me to have a judgment about her skills. THIS is an example of subjective, not objective! Subjective includes when you hone in on some mistake that you've made that other people didn't even notice. She had an inner picture of an ideal and in her opinion she didn't achieve it. But that was her own opinion, it was not based on facts.

The great irony here is that you are probably a real critical thinker in other areas of your life but not when it comes to your own self-evaluation. You might be great at discerning how much time to budget to get a project done, what your family members do and don't need when you are out shopping, or the points to make or leave out on a pitch deck. You often show that skill for other people. But are you directing it toward your own self-evaluation?

A close friend of mine from college is a highly capable lawyer. When her daughter shows my friend's same brand of perfectionism, she's able to reflect her daughter's talents and not dwelling on flaws.

But when my friend judges herself because she doesn't think she is doing a 'good enough' job in her work, she loses objectivity. One night her husband asked her: *"Who* do you think *is* doing a better job?" She was a speechless deer in the headlights, caught not being objective! She couldn't think of anyone who was doing it better. In fact, all she could see is how the clients often come to her because she is the one with answers that are the most fact –based and contextualized. You want to borrow your strength to help you be objective when it comes to yourself. You want to learn how to shift from self-critical to critical thinker.

Here are 3 strategies to help you apply the mantra of Be Objective.

1. Distinguish what you could know from what you need to know *now*

Ever criticized yourself saying "I don't know enough. Other people know more than me". If so, you probably imagine the full universe of all the things there is to know about a certain subject and then focus on the gap of what you don't know. "I don't know everything so I can't speak on that; I can't tell my clients I offer that service because I don't have a formal credential; or I can't try to influence on this in my company because what if they call me on it." That's subjective, and vague. That means you still have some homework to do. Instead you want to become more objective.

Identify "What is the full universe of things someone could know about this subject? And distinguish that from "What is mission critical for ME to know in order to get a result now?"

Then *get busy* knowing that! Instead of listening to the obnoxious roommate in your head, close the door and put your time, energy, and attention into studying! Figure out "What is the most important thing for me to know now, or what do I need to know next in order to get a result?"

Even gaining clarity on the distinction between what you could know and what will help you to know now is a good use of your time. If you can 'wing it' and feel comfortable entering a situation without knowledge, then all the better – go for it (many women will quip that now you know how some men operate!) But women generally benefit from feeling prepared and having knowledge – that's all good. Just be more strategic in where you put your time and energy. Once you know enough to get a result you will feel more confident. And then that will reveal the next topics or skills you need to know.

And you should feel free to set clear expectations with others about what you can and can't do for them. Often, we feel afraid of saying we don't know something because we think we should know everything, and that's not being discerning about what's within your scope to know well, and what is a separate arena. You want to have the confidence to say, "I can help you with part A, but for part B I am either going to have to do some research, or else let's pull in another resource who has that specific skillset." That makes you credible.

Here's an example of how to apply this idea of Be Objective: My client was a consultant on the diversity team at a pharma company. She had a proposal for a company policy but was hesitating to speak up, believing she "didn't know enough." When we did this exercise, she identified a handful of key reports that would be helpful to familiarize herself with and summarize in order to make the case for a policy she wanted to recommend. Rather than being overwhelmed by pressuring herself to know every report within the field (and thus not taking action), she became specific about the 3 points she needed to data justification for. She poured herself into that specific subject, and within a few weeks felt a sense of mastery. THEN she confidently presented her arguments and successfully gained buy-in for the proposed policy. As she started to connect with her Horizon Point (her inner persona of fabulousness she simply called "Carmen!") she felt emboldened to apply for a lead role on the diversity team…and got it!   (Epilogue: When she brought me in to train her company's high potential women leaders, she was bold enough to share that story with her colleagues, and got a whooping cheer!)

Women business owners often face this block when considering 'putting themselves' out there. Whether it's about doing a speech or writing a blog, or offering a service that you may not have been specifically trained in, you can apply this idea. Natasha is in my program where business owners become the Go To Expert in their field. She is early in her career and felt intimidated at the idea of giving a speech because she doesn't have as much experience as other financial advisors and is still in the process of getting her financial planning degree. Getting objective helped her.

We broke it down: What is the universe of things you will want to learn over your career vs what does your prospect need to know now that you can teach them? What do you already know now that you can act on to get a client a result?   That enabled her to organize a seminar on budgeting for women who wanted to start a family. Her audience members found these basics extremely helpful - and 2 of them became her clients.

Information is being generated so rapidly and the pool of things to know is so vast that it's impossible for anyone to know everything these days, even people who are subject matter experts. That's why you want to develop your critical thinking. What if you had the tools to ask the right questions and frame the issues in ways that break down complexity? Then you'd have confidence to be pulled into any situation and feel like you could do an effective intake, scope the situation, and set a path forward even if you don't know much of the specific issues - because you know how to think critically and ask good questions. (To develop this skill, I highly recommend www.Vervago.com as the best resource.)

2. Defang your Doubt

Is there anywhere in your life you are ambitious to break through the next level, but you're not going for it? Then this is the exercise for you! Whenever you are blocked it's a sign there's an argument going on with that obnoxious roommate in your head. She questions and criticizes you, she is the voice of your perceived weakness: "Are you really smart enough? Can you do that without failing? You're too old/young. You don't have that degree". You want to go for it but usually you believe her enough to question and block yourself. Then you are caught in a loop. Are you ready to take a stand and not allow yourself to get into that loop with her anymore?

Let's start by bringing a little objectivity into your argument, shall we?

First, your obnoxious roomate's arguments are vague. Usually they are something along the lines of "You're not smart enough" or "You're not a good presenter", etc. That's not helpful to you, no customer service department could take on such a vague complaint.

To get objective, here's step 1. Take that perceived weakness and break it down into component parts you can do something about. For example, if your roommate says, "You're not a good public speaker" you'd deconstruct what that means. Does that mean:

- "I'm soft spoken so I don't project loudly"
- "I don't know how to tell charismatic stories that engage the audience"
- I spend too much time reading the slide and not enough eye contact
- "I am fine on the presentation but freeze on hard questions"

What exactly does "not a good speaker" mean? Require you and your roommate to get really clear in your discussion.

Second, you will now make a choice to finally do something about each component of that perceived weakness. Here are the two choices. Either you will Accept that aspect of your perceived weakness is kind of true about you. Or you will Accomplish the skills to make it no longer true about you. (See Diagram 7)

If you **Accept**, it means you will not keep beating yourself up expecting yourself to be better at this perceived weakness. **Accept** involves focusing on your strengths and making a valuable contribution through them. It might require workarounds or hiring/partnering with someone who has the ability you don't. For example, if you are an introvert it might mean orienting your business around influencing through blogs rather than public speaking. Or being really good at running the team but partnering with an extrovert to be the face of the business.

OR you're going to **Accomplish**. That means you decide the perceived weakness is a skill that is mission critical for you to have in order to have the success and contribution you want to make. And maybe you do need to become better at that skill in order to make your mark. So, you would make a plan and commit to **Accomplish** learning that skill, whatever it takes! You might get a coach, take a training, etc. and set up a plan with accountability. That way you are assured that within a designated period of time, this will no longer be an issue for you.

You can do Either **Accept**, or **Accomplish**, or sometimes a combination of both.

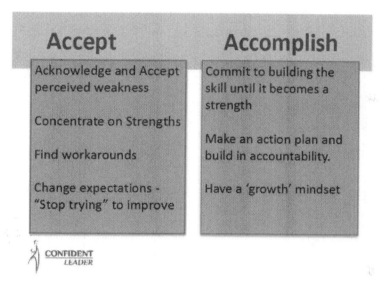

Diagram 7

Here's an example from a woman who did "C-school". She was a manager of a team of subject matter experts in a financial institution. Her confidence wobbled because she didn't have the technical expertise of her reports. Here's how she worked it out:

She **Accepted** her role. She got clear on what she needed to do to advance the work and advance herself in the organization. She Accepted that she didn't have to know everything that her subject matter experts knew. She reminded herself that her role was to **manage** and she's really good all the things a manager does to coordinate projects, mentor, etc. She re-engaged with managing and made sure her team was high-performing.

At the same time, she recognized that in order to project manage effectively, it would be helpful to know a little more about the guts of the coding process – such as details and bugs that would affect timelines. Similarly, she now saw herself as the translator between her group and other parts of the company that were pressuring her group for turnaround times. So, there was some jargon she needed to know. Therefore, she also did a strategy of **Accomplish** - put together a tutorial process for herself. She read parts of blogs that brought her up to speed; she had some of her team members teach her about key terminology; she took a mini- course. And within a matter of weeks she felt much more confident. She took these newfound approaches into her regular cross functional project meetings and the big boss complimented her on how she was showing up as a leader. She was able to advocate more effectively for her team, and was better able to serve the needs of the business. A win-win because she didn't stay stuck in her self-doubting loop. She prevailed in her argument with her obnoxious roommate!

3. Quantify your value to know your worth

You want to get feedback from others in order to know how well you are serving the needs and delivering the value that has been mutually agreed upon. Again, this is the distinction between Indirect and Go Direct. Indirect strategies are an effort to get other people to help you regulate your confidence. Go Direct is you are coming from a place of confidence and being open to others feedback to continually learn and improve your contribution.

Especially when it comes to matters concerning compensation, women can undervalue themselves. *We think about what we should earn according to our filters of 'not good enough' or not as good as… instead of about the objective value we provide.*

You want to be objective about the value you provide. Here's an exercise to do that.

If you run your own business, use a 4-column chart to determine the value your client receives from your services. This chart enables you to see not only the actual results you helped the client get, but also what are the tangible and intangible benefits of those results for your clients (or your boss, your group, your company, etc) as well as all the people in their life.

I'll first give an example of how I could fill out this chart about valuing services to one of my clients (who is a business owner):

Result	Intangible Benefits	Who and What Else Benefits	Intangible Benefits
Extra $50,000 net in 4 months	Child's private school, mother in apt nearby, less stress	Improved power balance and housework sharing with husband	Happier marriage and home life
Freedom from self-critical inner voice	Less stressed Sleeping through night Healthy Energy Poised not yelling with children	Children getting needed attention for school issues	Positive family relationships Children thriving in school
Hired 2 new employees	Team less stressed, More work accomplished	Higher level target market – earns more per client. Increased revenue	Positive work environment, less turnover
2 afternoons with children	Freedom from parenting guilt	Improved work life balance	Improved relationship with children

You can see how much more broad this client's gains are then just the external results. For example, she reduced the stress and increased the closeness of all relationships in the family for the rest of her children's time in the home. What is that worth to a client?? If you are a business owner considering the value you bring and what fees to charge, you want to take into consideration this wholistic picture because that is the full value your service provides.

Even if you just take it to the 2nd column it still broadens your thinking. Here's an example I could fill in about one of my corporate clients:

Result: Got a promotion to a next level role	Benefits: Cessation of frustration; Reduced stress on family; Raise; Increased job satisfaction;
Increased responsibility More say in the organization	-Aligned with talents; Job satisfaction -Influence from her 'listening tour' - Increase network and positioning for future roles
Eliminated doubt about public speaking – spoke on 2 panels in 6 months	-Visibility in her field; expands options/ network for future role - Attended a conference in Europe and got to bring husband for vacation Attended a conference in Europe and brought husband for a vacation

If you are in the corporate world you can still do a variation on this chart. You want to do this before you make any "Ask" for greater responsibility or resources or salary.

What are your accomplishments is a good place to start. Those are usually answers to the first column "results you have achieved". But also consider how have you brought value to the business? What is your unique contribution? Are there ideas you contributed? Did you accelerate completion of a project? Have you taken leadership of an initiative? Are your social skills that glue that keeps the team engaged? Write it down! (And then find out information about the salary range in the market and potentially amongst your colleagues.)

What's holding you back – Is it Doubt, or is it Bias?

There is a commonly cited internal study by Hewlett Packard which indicates that men will apply for a job if they have only 6/10 qualifications while women believe they need to have all 10. The implication is that women are perfectionists and need more confidence to feel ready for next level roles. Upon further analysis, this might not be the case. Tara Mohr, author of *Playing Big: Practical Wisdom for Women Who Want to Speak Up, Create, and Lead,* [iv] was curious about the finding and surveyed 1000 American professionals.[v] She found that the most frequent reason both men and women didn't apply for jobs was "I didn't think they'd hire me since I didn't meet the qualifications and I didn't want to waste my time." She also found that women didn't want to apply because they didn't want to fail and they saw themselves as merely following the hiring guidelines – whereas men were much less likely to have these concerns.

In other words, women took the requirements literally and didn't see the hiring process as one where effective advocacy or relationship building could create a possible future for them. Her conclusion was that the most effective fix would be to make the hiring process more transparent for all employees, including women.

And that if there is a confidence issue for women, it seems to follow the idea of 'skinned knee' socialization. A good lesson would be to not consider the hiring process a strict 'play by the rules' system. Apply anyway – you never know what conversation it can catalyze. For example, Magda applied for an analytical position in a financial institution even though the group to which she applied had always had an all-male staff. Even though she didn't get the position, it triggered a series of career conversations with her manager, and now she is being groomed for a promotion within her current group.

Though you want to use the strategies in chapter 6 to 'go for it,' women's perceptions can have validity in an environment where bias is at play. Women sometimes do have to have greater qualifications than men, stemming from a performance bias whereby men's promotion is based on criteria of future performance whereas women's is based on past track record. As part of their education, women are rewarded for rule following yet can pay a cost once in the workplace. Women often need better credentials in order to prove their competence and may overemphasize certain certifications or formal skills while underutilizing networking and effective influence. Women also may get nervous about negotiating because they intuit – correctly – that self-advocating for higher pay would reduce the essential leadership ingredient (their 'likeability'). (Fortunately, this social response to women is eliminated when women negotiate on behalf of others, a 'focus on your end user' strategy). (See Chapter 13 for more information about how to deal with Bias.)

The great irony of this chapter on being objective is that a frequent refrain I hear from women is that "facts should matter." Women feel objectivity is diluted in an 'old boys club' culture: "Promotions and the best accounts shouldn't be doled out based on favoritism or who you play golf with, it should be based on merit." We want to all contribute to a culture of objectivity and merit, then we must be Impeccable for our 50% and be objective as well! (See Chapter 13 for more information about how to deal with Bias.)

Another big can of worms is the controversy that was symbolized by the positions of Sheryl Sandberg vs Anne Marie Slaughter over whether women need to be more confident to 'lean in' and/or whether our society needs to support families so that women have bandwidth for greater responsibility. For each individual woman, the answer might be one, the other, or both. For example, I was speaking for women sales agents at a large financial institution and the organizers asked me to help the women be more confident to take on sales manager roles. What I heard from the women is that they enjoyed the control they currently had and didn't want the life they currently saw portrayed in the management role. When I talked with the women further, I heard it was both. Each woman has to 'diagnose' what the blocks are for her – take responsibility for being 'ready and willing'. And similarly, organizations need to be responsive to the needs of men and women who are seeking greater control and flexibility for their lives.

In sum, whenever you notice that you are criticizing yourself, it's a sign that you are caught in your own filters. You want to cultivate the practice of shifting from Subjective to Objective.

POINTS TO REMEMBER

- Shift from Subjective (opinion, your filters) to Objective (fact based)
- Instead of "I don't know enough" distinguish what you *could* know from what you need to know now to get a result.
- Require yourself to Be Objective about your perceived weakness – either Accept and work around them, or get busy to Accomplish an upskilling.
- When tempted to undervalue your worth, quantify your value to the client/organization to see your full value.
- Request specific and objective input from those who offer only vague feedback where bias flourishes.
- Use your capacity to love to have courage and act as a steward of your 'End Users'
- See yourself as an equal rather than judge yourself 'below' others, that makes you anxious
- Are you a worrier? Channel your worry into understanding the needs of your end user.

NEXT STEPS

- Download and print out some of the exercises in this chapter at **www.doubtfreenow.com**
- If you want me to help you shift from self-critical to critical thinker, find out more at **www.sharonmelnick.com**

Chapter 8:
From Reactive to Respected:
Respond Powerfully Instead of Taking Things Personally (Even in the Face of People with Strong Energy)

"When you look at the challenges of being a change-maker and being willing to buck the establishment, it's important to learn how to take criticism seriously but not personally, and to do that you have to be willing to hear what others who are your critics are saying and to evaluate where they are coming from."

-Hillary Clinton,

U.S. Senator, Secretary of State, Presidential Candidate

Imagine you are driving your car in a shopping mall parking lot and the driver behind you honks his horn and, at the exact same moment, your cellphone rings. Immediately, without thinking, where do you go in your mind?

- Jerk! He was unjustifiably impatient and aggressive.

- I must be doing something wrong. I better figure out what it is.

- It was an accident; his child probably bumped the horn while playing in the front seat.

- He was giving a helpful traffic communication; let me see if my tail light is out.

- -It had nothing to do with me; he trying to catch the attention of his wife leaving the store

- He genuinely had an emergency and needed to pass me quickly.

The explanation – or 'story' – you tell about the 'facts' in each situation will entirely determine your behavior in that situation. Think the guy is a jerk? You might curse into the rear-view mirror, deliberately slam on your brakes, and pick up the phone with a tone. (Note: at least, this is the first response of many New Yorkers. Though a generalization, I've asked thousands of people this question and those in the 'nice' Midwest of the United States tend to ascribe a helpful explanation!) Think you might have done something wrong? You might ignore the ringing phone as you wave an apology... and your mood, interpersonal behavior, will set up the next moment, and the one after that.

What most of us do is take our stories and make them into 'facts.' Indeed, I bet you'll drive home from the shopping mall parking lot that afternoon and call your spouse or best friend and say, "When I was at the mall today, a guy was such a jerk" or "When I was at the mall today, I almost caused a little traffic snafu." And that will turn into your history of the day. I bet none of you will think "When I was at the mall today, some guy honked his horn *and what I made of it was . . .*" You probably won't realize the power you have to invent your own reality.

Horns are honking all day long in your work and personal life. With each interaction and event that occurs, you have an opportunity to respond. Do you take it personally and react? Do you get defensive and have a tone? Or do you show up confident and objective at your Horizon Point? Your reaction comes from the 'story' – the explanations, interpretations - you tell about the facts.

In this chapter, you will learn how to NOT REACT. How to be rational instead of reactive, how to respond powerfully instead of taking things personally. You will learn to take the emotionality out of situations and keep them fact-based. Most people do not do this so you will always be able to be a calm role model. It will help you not have to rehash situations with regret afterwards if you became defensive. Even though, every day, emotions are present in the workplace and are the main source of motivation, you also want to Be Impeccable for your 50% – do your part to not feed into stereotypes about women as being "emotional."

(As an aside, my favorite response to women being accused of being emotional was Carly Fiorina, former CEO of Hewlett Packard, who was being interviewed by Katie Couric as she launched her brief presidential candidacy campaign. When asked about how she responds to concerns about a woman in the White House being affected by hormones, she replied "I think we've seen plenty of evidence of men in the White House making decisions based on their hormones!")

Having confidence in the heat of the moment protects you from reacting. What's the connection? When you have a doubt about yourself, it creates uncertainty – am I enough, or not? Do I belong in this role, or not? Am I smart enough for this client to hire me, or not? You are wired to try to create a sense of certainty, especially about a matter so fundamental to your core security. If you don't have that rock-solid confidence from within, you will oscillate between many moments you might feel confident and others where you can't access it. You will do what it takes to try to answer that underlying question once and for all. Following the idea of the Indirect path framework, if you are not sourcing your confidence from within, you will look to people and events that happen in order to get the answer.

That's why you are other-directed. That's why it matters to you what other people think. Because what they say – or don't say – is the information you will use to answer the question of whether you are 'enough'. This personalizing of people's behavior in situations is what sets you up to REACT!

I notice that 'taking things personally' is extremely common. I hear it all the time, even when I am training or coaching a group of more senior women who are confident more often than not. This skill is highly relevant for all confidence types. Indeed, it happens to the best of us!

When I moved to NYC 12 years ago, I subcontracted as an executive coach for one of the marquis recruitment and leadership firms. I had been introduced to the firm through a friend and was hoping to grow my engagements with them so I could build my practice in NYC. Midway through an engagement, I receive the startling news that my client had been fired. That had never happened to me before. The next day, I get an email from the administrative assistant to the head of the coaching group at the big firm, wanting to set up a conference call. So, what do I immediately think? I explained the fact of my client getting fired as due to: "I did wrong. I let things fall through the cracks." Then I played out fearful scenarios in my mind that "I too would be fired." I reacted.

I was upset that I was in jeopardy of losing the future business. I could barely sleep for several nights. And then my phone meeting with the 'big cheese' was postponed for three weeks . . . three weeks of torturous anticipation!

Finally, we get on the phone and what does she say? "I only have 5 minutes on my way to the airport but wanted to know if you would coach a dear personal friend of mine who is stuck; I've heard raves about your work." I breathe for the first time in 3 weeks. All that time wasted, all of that emotional churn – for nothing! Then I call the firm and find out my client was terminated because of statements she had made a year before that could have been a liability to the company – i.e., it had NOTHING to do with me! I could have found that information out weeks before but I didn't act constructively because I was so convinced it was *because of my flaws*.

Dozens of times a day, horns honk and you have to explain to yourself 'why' in order to know how to act. It's not pathological to 'tell stories'; our human faculty to interpret facts is what differentiates us from animals who act on instinct. Know this: **The stories you tell will determine the quality of your life and leadership.**

What's the fix? Apply your ability to Be Objective. Here's a 5-column method you can use to prevent yourself from reacting in the heat of the moment.

I knew Jana through the "C-school" program. She was a few years into her career and worked in a small company that services clients' financial needs. She receives an email alert about a trade she conducted. As a Perfectionist/Criticizer she immediately 'reacts.' She panics and blames herself. She tells herself she's stupid. She drops the work she's doing and spends 90 minutes investigating what the mistake was and, most relevant to her – whether SHE made it.

Let's use the 5-column chart to see how Jana learned to not REACT or take it personally. (See Diagram 8)

Column 1: Fact or Event

In this column, simply mark down the fact or event that triggered the reaction. Make sure to identify a *fact* and not be inferential. For example, 'he stole my idea' is not a fact. "He repeated the same idea I described 15 minutes after I did in a meeting" is a fact.

"I receive an email that informs of an ALERT about a trade I made"

Column 2: Lead Story

In this column, note 'where you go in your mind.' This column is your unexamined, gut response that explains 'why' the fact happened.

"I screwed up royally; it was my mistake."

In order to get rapid insight from this exercise, do the 'dig down.' You identify what your lead story means about you. This step helps you immediately see how you are personalizing the situation.

Ask the dig down question: "What does it mean *about you* that you "screwed up royally"?

"It means 'I am stupid'."

Here we have Jana's real lead story. Even though the facts of the situation are that a generic email alert about a trade arrived in her inbox, her gut explanation for why that fact happened is that it was because of her own inabilities. Though it sounds farfetched, in her mind, it's as if she was sent an email with the subject line: "Jana you are stupid!"

That is why Jana reacted. The email activated a judgment she has about herself. The power of her response came from this triggering of her doubt. Notice that she takes on all the blame and makes the faulty trade 'all about her.'

Most of us tell our Lead Story (unexamined gut reaction) about a situation and then think we have fully understood that situation. And then we turn our stories into facts. We walk away from the situation confirming the assumptions we jumped to – in this case, it's "I'm stupid" but in the honking situation, it could be "he's a jerk." And then we go down the negative rabbit hole – beating ourselves up, reinforcing a doubt and finding ourselves at a dead end with nowhere to go but self-flagellate, hide, wallow, or try to redeem ourselves by getting someone to compliment us (notice the parallels to the Indirect path patterns).

Stories Log

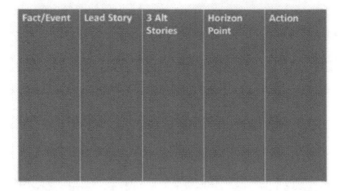

Fact/Event	Lead Story	3 Alt Stories	Horizon Point	Action

Diagram 8

Column 3: Three Alternative Stories

Column 3 is where you start to learn a new skill. You are required to tell three alternative stories about why that fact happened before you are allowed to act.

Jana's alternative stories:

1. The alert had nothing to do with the part of the trade that I worked on.

2. I carried out the trade according to the instructions of my manager so, if there was a mistake, it was in the directions given to me.

3. I made a benign operational or logistical error and this was the notification to correct it so the trade could easily go through – i.e., I did make a mistake but it's a mistake that is easily kept in perspective.

4. I misunderstood the client's request.

Notice that in column 3, you start to understand more about the actual context in which the trade was ordered and executed.

Column 4: Your Horizon Point

In Column 4, you remind yourself of who you want to be at your Horizon Point, and maybe some of the qualities or attributes that are important for you to show up with.

Jana wants to be someone with unwavering confidence who moves forward from situations. Important quality: Confident

The skill is to CHOOSE the story or combination of stories that enable you to show up as your Horizon Point. In this case, Jana chose the story that it was probably a minor logistical error and would be easily corrected. It wasn't about her stupidity.

Column 5: Your response

Column 5 is where you decide and act on your response.

Notice that when Jana stayed stuck in her original lead story, it led her actions in Column 5 to be two hours of panicky investigation as to whether she made the fateful mistake and worrying about it's consequences. In the process of her investigation, she informed a number of people about the alert and thus widely announced her perceived mistake. She didn't learn anything from the situation because she was convinced it was her fault, and if a similar email alert happens the following week, she will have a similar response.

If she chooses the story where it was probably a minor logistical error, her response would have been: Finish working on the task I'm working on and not drop it. Don't announce it to everyone. Find out what the error was, and how it was made. Note the learnings so I don't make the mistake again. Then get back to work after a few minutes!

Compare Jana's actions that stemmed from her Lead Story (lose two hours of productivity and drain emotional energy) to actions that stemmed from her alternative story (new learning, continuous focus and productivity). These two responses are like night and day in terms of her learning and productivity. Your response is the only thing that people interacting with you see, but it is based on the thinking you do in Columns 1-4.

Here's another example with Nikki's 'Stories' log. She used it to stay poised and be collaborative

Fact/Event:

I ask the compliance people in my company for a waiver so they can conduct certain experiments that will help us refine a drug in a country in Asia. The compliance people say, "we can't give the waiver you asked for."

Lead Story:

- They are stupid and lazy.

Dig Down: "And what does that mean about you?"

- They are setting me up to do a bad job. *That means I'm not good at my job.*

Alternative Stories:

1. They didn't fully understand my request.
2. This is an unusual 'out of the box' request they are not used to or trained for so they didn't know what else to say.
3. I didn't walk them through sufficient context to show them that it could be easier than they thought it would be.

Horizon Point:

"The Pilot": calm and in control of herself – the one who guides people through the stormy part of the skies and leads the way toward collaborative solutions.

Action:

When she was stuck in her "Lead story," she got frustrated and told them they needed to find a solution. (Then her manager told her she needed to deal with the situation with less of a 'tone'!)

She felt bad about herself that she snapped.

With her alternative story: The next time she gets frustrated because she sees people as lazy, she will instead ask structuring questions that help them tap their problem solving. She'll do more to 'make them the hero' so they are motivated to help her find a solution. Such as: "Let's talk it through. Can you tell me what you've done before when presented with this kind of commercial situation...? Would it be possible to...?" We discussed how to bring others along to catch up to her thinking.

Here's an example of how Linda applied the Stories log to learn how to not REACT the next time she is with friends.

Fact/Event:

Linda goes to a dinner party at a friend's house. During the time of the evening that everyone is serving their dinner at the buffet and getting a drink, some of the women are talking. Lisa is asked about her recent vacation and starts telling a story about it, during which time three of the women either talk over her or walk away from her.

Lead Story:

"They are rude."

Dig Down:

"And what does it mean about YOU that they are rude?"

It means that I don't matter.

Alternative Stories:

1.   They are not real and true friends; they are acquaintances so they don't have that level of interest in my vacation

2.   The time of the evening in which I was invited to tell my vacation story disrupted my story – everyone was still up and down getting drinks and we hadn't yet settled into our places and stayed put to eat dinner

3.   I wasn't as concise as I could have been in getting to the punch line of my story.

Horizon Point:

"Cool, calm, and confident."   Someone who owns her value and feels deserving.

She CHOSE the story that everyone hadn't settled into the seating area yet and was still in flux, making it a distracting time to tell an involved story.

Action:

When she was stuck in her "Lead Story," she shut down, stopped talking, and was resentful of her friends.

With her alternative story: She said next time she would pay more attention to the context and wait to tell a story; she said she might ask if people were interested in hearing all the details – or not - and tell the story according to the input. She even said she was going to pay more attention to her friendships and whether she felt they were a good fit for her and how she could increase the number of friends she felt at ease with.

What are takeaways from the Stories log method? This exercise gives you a practical method you can use 'in the heat of the moment' to reframe the situation and instead act in the service of your Horizon Point.

Comparing how each exemplar reacted when they were stuck in their Lead Story vs when they told an Alternative Story about the situation is illuminating. Across each example, the women were able to be more productive and bring a better solution to everyone involved. Jana got a better result for herself by saving time and learning more for next time. Nikki would get a better result for the company by working with her colleagues in compliance to come up with a solution for the business AND she would strengthen her relationship with them for the next time the business needs a creative solution. Linda would feel more empowered, would have more fulfilling interpersonal interaction and would be motivated to make sure she is surrounding herself with people who increase her sense of joy.

In each of these examples, you can see that the Lead Story is a negative conviction the woman has about herself. You react because this core belief becomes activated – seemingly out of the blue – before you even know it is happening. Automatically, you feel on the defensive. What sends you down the negative spiral are two features of your Lead Story: Either it's "personalizing" (e.g., my client getting fired was about my lack of competence) or it's "globalizing." Globalizing simply means that you make an all-encompassing, black and white assertion such as "the compliance people are lazy" or "I'm not smart enough." No person or situation is either all good or all bad, so your Lead Story should alert you that you could look at the situation more objectively (aka, tell an alternative story!)

The 'dig down' part of the exercise is a high-speed train to identify the core belief that might be holding you back and causing you to react. Usually, this belief is longstanding and developed as part of your adaptation to circumstances earlier in your life. The 'part' of you that carries the beliefs and feelings of this negative belief gets activated with your Lead Story – that's why you feel hijacked. It takes over the rest of the thinking parts of you with it's intense concerns.

What do I have to do to 'get rid of' my negative voice so I won't react again? The "stories" method is a helpful tool to act with more intention in the moment. However, if you've had a 'negative voice' about yourself for as long as you can remember, it's like kindling ready to get activated and make you react. Practical 'in the moment' strategies like 'telling a different story' are very helpful, but they don't 'clean' up the trigger at its source. They won't erase your longstanding 'negative voice' that keeps hijacking you to feel 'not enough'. So, it can still be effortful to keep having to tell alternative stories in each new situation.

Usually, the complete solution is to change your longstanding belief at its source - and then be armed with the stories log for the times moments catch you off guard. There is a 'secret sauce' technique I developed in my research at Harvard Medical School that traces your 'negative voice' back to its origin and roots it out at its source.

The results are that you simply 'don't go to that place of reaction anymore", you naturally feel 'free' of doubt and criticism and fear. Clients who have done this single exercise report it is like having "a new lease on life", or that it gave them a "90% improvement" on their 'negative voice'. They say that afterward 'the sky is the limit' for them.

(This is an exercise I can only do xin an individual session, you can find out more about how we can erase your years of self-doubt with these techniques at **www.sharonmelnick.com/freedom** or contact me directly at **sharon@sharonmelnick.com**)

POINTS TO REMEMBER

- When you react, it comes from being stuck in an unexamined "Lead" story about the situation
- Require yourself to look at the situation from 3 differing perspectives before you allow yourself to act.
- Choose the explanations of situations that enable you to act at your Horizon Point
- People only see your outward behavior but the intentional thinking that you do in Columns 1-4 sets up your behavioral response.

NEXT STEPS

- Your field work is to log 3 situations using this 5-column chart to help you build the skill to Not React. You can download the chart at www.doubtfreenow.com
- If you notice that you are reactive and get hijacked, or if you know that you've had that 'negative voice' for as long as you can remember, there is a 'magic bullet' exercise that erases all those years of self-doubt and criticism, and 'heals' the 'part' of you the reaction comes from. You'll find you 'don't go there anymore' and feel liberated of the weight of that doubt, fear, or criticism. We do this in an individual session. If this is of interest to you, find out more about you can do this exercise directly with me at **http://www.sharonmelnick.com/freedom** or **contact me directly at sharon@sharonmelnick.com**

Chapter 9:
From Perfectionism to Peace of Mind:
How to Have Excellence (From Yourself and Others) Without Exhaustion

"Understanding the difference between healthy striving and perfectionism is critical to laying down the shield and picking up your life. Many people think of perfectionism as striving to be your best, but it is not about self-improvement; it's about earning approval and acceptance. Perfectionism is a self-destructive and addictive belief system that fuels this primary thought: 'If I look perfect, and do everything perfectly, I can avoid or minimize the painful feelings of shame, judgment, and blame.' Research shows that perfectionism hampers success. In fact, it's often the path to depression, anxiety, addiction, and life paralysis."

- Brené Brown, Author of The Gifts of Imperfection

It must be confusing to hear that you have to 'let go of your perfectionism.' That's the least helpful thing you can tell a perfectionist! You'll think: "But that's what's gotten me to my level of success. That's part of my personal brand. I'm appreciated because my clients and team can count on me. They know that I'll go the extra mile and that everything will be prepared. Even though I'm kind of tired, there's the joy of a job well-done and I'm willing to sacrifice for that."

You are results-oriented so I'll cut to the chase: The skill you will develop in this chapter is how to have objectivity so you know the difference between healthy striving and perfection. Know when your perfectionism crosses over a threshold where its stress exceeds its benefit. What does it look like when it's crossed the line? If you've exhausted yourself all year making sure that nothing fell through the cracks, you were the go-to person and executor of the team's important initiatives . . . but then you were passed over for promotion because you were 'too in the details' and not 'strategic' enough. Or have you put all your energy into running your business and making sure that it was giving great service, but you didn't think of what's the next step or the next level, and now you feel stuck? And then you tell yourself you should have taken on a new service or a new strategy, or you didn't train someone else to do it so you have to be the one who keeps doing it. That's the frustration that I want you to avoid by being aware of this perfectionism cycle and freeing yourself from it. This chapter is especially relevant for Perfectionist/Criticizer, but is relevant for any Performer or Confident Leader as well.

You want to get off the Perfection cycle and onto the cycle of Productivity with Peace of Mind. (See Diagram 9)

Get off the Perfectionist Cycle

Diagram 9

When you pressure yourself to be perfect, it creates stress. A stress reaction is composed of three parts. In your physiology, you will feel pressure, overstimulation, or freneticism. In your psychology, you will think "I have to be perfect. I need to push myself. What are people going to think about me?" – which, as we know, is an Indirect Path concern. In your performance, your approach will be: "I need to do it all now; I need to be the one to do it all because no one will do it as well as me." Then you over-focus on the details, and do and redo the work. You will multi-task. Yes, women have a greater capacity to multi-task then men, but just because you *can* doesn't mean you *should* (it leads to a 33% degradation in efficiency and little to no working memory). You might react to any little mistake, or you might have a knee-jerk response if anything has to change. You might be impatient with others who aren't as quick or don't share your vision for how the work should get done.

As we know Indirect Path behaviors create a vicious cycle – the more perfectionism is your primary mode, the more you will need it to remain your primary mode. So, let's break the stress cycle. Here are three strategies – one in each of the domains of the stress reaction. First, your physiology, followed by your psychology, and finally your performance.

Strategy #1: Balance your On and your Off buttons.

I thought it would be helpful to take a page from my book and trainings on *Success Under Stress*. It has many strategies to help you to concentrate and prioritize in moments of overwhelm. Here is one of the many strategies you can use to get off the Perfectionism cycle.

We have two parts to our nervous system, which is the part of our body that responds to relentless demand and the constant change. Our "On" button gives us focus and energy to solve problems and run from meeting to meeting. Our "Off" button gives us calm and rejuvenation. We're supposed to have coordination between the On button and the Off button. When we were evolving early in our history and that saber-toothed tiger was running at us, we might have a full blown "On" button 'fight or flight' response. But then, later in the day, we could be found in the dark cave resting, digesting, maintaining our immune system, making cave paintings. But the way that we live now, there's no balance between the On and Off button; we are always On.

That has consequences for our thinking and our confidence. The On button has a mode of thinking associated with it. It's very reactive to demands we have to deal with – an email comes in or somebody knocks at your door, or you're called on in a meeting, or you have to present in front of your network, or there's some problem that you have to deal with and your "On" activates automatically to deal with it. Your "On" button mode of thinking is tactical. Thinking is short-term and black and white. Your "On" button mode of thinking can only reference the past or the ways that you responded to the situation in the past. Innovation is not the brainchild of your On button mode of thinking! This is not the mode of thinking that's going to help you to have new self-talk.

The On button is a survival mechanism. It's all about me, myself, and mine, so you will be tempted to stay stuck in your "Lead stories" and see the situation through the lens of "What does mean about me? What's the implication for my team or my resources?" Your On button is needed to carry out tactics; you just need to know what its limitations are. Obviously where I'm going with this is that you want to balance it with your Off button thinking. Your Off button thinking gives you access to the big picture. It helps you to connect the dots. It helps you to synthesize information that you've been hearing from conferences, from networking events, from your meetings across functions, etc. So, it helps you tap your creativity and your intuition; it helps you see things more objectively and see things that are coming down the pike so that you can have new ideas. This is what helps you see for the long term and to be strategic. Your On button is engaged all day long without your having to put effort into it, but you really have to do something to press the Off button so you access that synthesizing kind of thinking that's going to make you smart.

There are strategies in the book or online versions of *Success Under Stress* to balance your On and Off buttons. (There are techniques you can do to balance your On and Off button within 1-3 minutes during your busy overwhelming days that will help you concentrate and also put you back to sleep within 3 minutes when you awaken at 2 am thinking about your 'to do' list. Find out more at www.sharonmelnick.com/sus)

You want to learn to set aside time for Off button thinking or what I'm calling 'connect the dots time' in your schedule. We all want to have that quality time to reflect and 'think' but unless you designate time, it's unlikely you will ever finish your 'to do' items and get around to it. Go Direct is about being proactive. Schedule "Off" button thinking or connect the dots time and use that time to lift off the perfection cycle and see things from the big picture perspective. Synthesize the things that you've been hearing to come up with new ideas, to look at things from new angles. Ask yourself: "Where do I want my career/business to go? What are the trends and how could I bring more value to my End User? How might I differentiate myself from other people who are also in my role or other people who offer my business or services?" This kind of thinking makes you smarter, which is going to help you feel more confident to speak up, put yourself out there and be seen as someone who is a go-to expert or someone to have at the table. Having time for this more reflective thinking will also calm your brain.

Strategy #2: Take Imperfect Action

Literally every thing that you see in the world started by someone taking imperfect action. Trying to figure it out in your head and put out a perfect first draft is "Indirect" (and uninformed!) Go Direct is being so focused on furthering a project or service to help your End User that you get it started. You learn from mistakes and constantly make it better. Follow the mantra "She who makes the most mistakes wins!"

Silicon Valley and the entrepreneurial spirit in our world has given us a new idea of 'failure'. Now entrepreneurs are not seen as seasoned unless they have risked and failed. We now have the tools to 'Fail Fast'. Put out your first iteration and get feedback from your clients and customers through online surveys and social media. Use 'big data' like response rates, conversion statistics, or sales numbers to know how to shape your ideas. If you are concerned about your colleague's or senior leaders' evaluations, circulate a first draft of your report with the label Confidential or Draft so others know it's a work in progress – Just don't put off getting it out!

You want to have a sense of perspective to stay focused on what's truly important. This book is a live example. I am sure there are still some mistakes in this book. Despite a lot of attention, a few typos will have escaped our notice and many places my writing could be more concise. I might hear from a few people about it (as I sometimes do after I post a blog). But let me ask you: are YOU getting enormous value from reading this book? Are you able to overlook the minor flaws and learn the information that could change the course of your life and career? Are you glad I focused on you as my End User and took imperfect action instead of getting shut down by the fear of how you will judge my typos and run-on sentences? THAT's what is important!

Strategy #3: Ask a different question.

Being "Always On" will derail from being objective. This next strategy has to do with your psychology – the way you think. Your brain will always answer the question you ask it, so Ask a different question! You've probably been asking the question about your project, or even your family member's birthday party: Is it perfect? As we know, that's an Indirect path question. Its translation is "what will people think about me," or "how can I make this perfect so that you compliment me or at all costs don't criticize and reject me?"

Instead, you might ask a question that helps you be objective. Here are three such questions. Answers to these questions will provide you with an objective purpose to your projects.

1. ***What's the purpose of the project I am working on?*** How do you determine the purpose? You could outline success criteria at the beginning of any project. You could identify what your End User will think or do when your project is complete. Ask yourself: Does the project fulfill its purpose now? If so, it's ready to hit 'send' and finish up. If not, then identify the specific gaps that remain and make a plan to fill those gaps.

Here's an example of defining your purpose could save a lot of stress: I arrived at a conference where I was giving the keynote speech. It was a technology company's women's leadership network client appreciation, and they had 100 guests from their client companies. Obviously, they wanted it to be high quality and memorable so it could foster relationships with their clients. The organizer was tense and kept nervously looking over the room and asking if everything looked ok. She asked me what I thought her boss would think of the room. To me, the room looked classy and well- organized, but that's not the point. Perfectionism is not objective. I was thinking it would be helpful if she could ask the question: "What's the purpose of the program?" The purpose was for the program to foster meaningful connections between her company and their clients, and amongst those clients – and to reflect their company's brand. The right question was whether the structure of the program, the set-up of the room, and the contents of the program book and keynote supported that end - not try to predict or control what her boss would think.

You want to develop awareness about the purpose behind your perfectionism. Sometimes it is objectively in the service of creating an outcome that will bring positive things to your End User and other times it's your own agenda. For example, do you have special gifts that make you an "artiste"? Are you a chef that wants the meal to turn out beautifully and for all the ingredients work together like a symphony? Are you an event planner who wants the details to help create a wow for the attendees? These are the 'right' reason to be a perfectionist –

because you are enjoying the ride and leveraging your talents. Or is it for the 'wrong' reasons – an Indirect path motivation to gain others' acceptance or prevent their criticism and rejection.

Start by being objective: what's the purpose of the project you're working on? If it fulfills the purpose, it's ready. If not, ask objectively what else will it need to get desired action, that's your game plan.

2. **What's the phase?** Know the phase – Instead of just pressuring yourself to make a project perfect, ask "**what phase are we in?**" and how will my perfectionism affect the timeline and quality of the work?

If you are in a brainstorming phase, your perfectionism is causing too much focus on detail and you might be experienced as a 'downer' to other people. Your perfectionism is more helpful during the planning and implementation phases. That's when you're going to have your eye on things that other people may not even see, and your perfectionism is going to be value add. You're going to optimize the project. You're going to have a vision of excellence that other people may not have because they were just trying to get it done. So, in the execution phase, your detail orientation may be very well-appreciated. As the decisions have already been made and it's time to get the project out the door, your perfectionism has passed the expiration date and better to throw it out.

3. **What's YOUR purpose?** You can guide your behavior by having clarity on your role on the project or what you are meant to bring to the situation. It helps to use your perfectionism in the area of your 'gift' or 'genius' but less so at other times.

For example, if you are hired as a professional organizer, you want your client's house to look as clean and orderly as you can make it so it provides a great energy. It's less important if it's your own kitchen on a weekday evening where you might use that time better on rejuvenating or quality time with your family. If you work in a creative profession, paying attention to the color or details of the design may be your 'gift' and you want to allow yourself the freedom to keep nurturing the process until the design is at its best – just like a chef, artist or fashion designer might fuss over the details until it fulfills their vision. Do you get a sense of joy from the aesthetics or how your user will experience it? If so, these would be considered the 'right' times to allow your energy to flow toward perfection. This is when perfectionism allows you to enjoy the ride. However, don't criticize yourself that it's not perfect yet; just keep making adjustments and enjoying the ride until 'it's perfect!'

On the other hand, if you are putting together your child's first birthday party, what's your purpose? Is it to make sure that all the banners are hung straight and napkins are perfectly folded? That probably won't be noticed by your 1-year-old, and if you are trying to impress the other parents, that might be considered an Indirect behavior. A poll by Working Mother magazine found that in 2013 working mothers #1 source of guilt was not the time spent with their children but the state of cleanliness of their house.[vi] If your purpose is to feel a better energy in the house, then find a cleaning solution. (If it's to impress other parents, that's Indirect - ask a different question!)

Strategy #4: Distinguish when your perfectionism is helpful and when harmful.

For this strategy, you want to bring more objectivity to the effects of your perfectionism on the project and on other people. You want to appreciate where your detail orientation and perfection adds value vs when your self-imposed pressure is harmful.

Sometimes the work does have to be exacting. Are you performing surgery or competing in the Olympics? Preparing the financials for a board meeting? Writing a law brief that cites 100 cases needing exact page numbers? Engineering parts for planes or the conductor of a train? Writing a TEDx talk that will be forever captured on video? Then let your inner perfectionist pony run free and keep working on it until it will get the desired result from the people using or watching your work. Go for it!

Develop an awareness of how your perfectionism affects the project and the other people you work with. Notice when you are being perfectionistic because you are telling yourself, "I should be perfect" or "this project needs to be perfect."

If you work with other people, know your perfectionism affects them and they may not share your need. Maybe they don't want to take extra time and go over deadline or redo things they consider details just so that YOU can feel ok about yourself. Are you aware of how others experience working with you? Are you aware of when it crosses the line from helpful to harmful?

If your perfectionism has been interfering with you having more of a presence online, as a speaker, or recognized expert, then get with the times! We now live in an age of transparency. 'Authenticity' is the new sexy. Your audience will not relate to you when you get up and try to act perfect and polished. They want to see you knowing your stuff but 'real' and 'vulnerable'. Then they know you've been there too and they can identify with you. Imagine if I wrote this book on Confidence from the vantage point of 'I'm perfect, you need to get your act together!' Would you be as receptive as when you know I said "No" to the White House and I've been all three Indirect confidence types so let me share with you what I've learned...

Require yourself to take a step back and decide "is my perfectionism helpful or harmful?" Fill out this chart with the next 5 times you notice yourself tempted to say, "it needs to be perfect" (it may take several days for you to get into 5 situations, or they may all happen today)

Use it to sort out: Where is my detail orientation, my perfection, helping to improve the product, or helping my clients to have trust in me that I absolutely have their back and going to catch everything and do what it takes for them. And where is it harmful?

	Helpful	Harmful
Situation 1		
Situation 2		
Situation 3		
Situation 4		
Situation 5		

And where it's harmful, then problem solve. Reduce the scope of the project. Choose subsections where perfectionism is helpful and others where it is not. Delegate where appropriate or start to develop people who work for you to think like you so, eventually, they can take over your functions and do it (nearly) as well as you do!

Make decisions about what work you will do from the perspective of who you want to be and what success you want to have, not from where you are and how you feel about yourself now.

Be intentional: Who do you want to be? What's the role that you want to play? What's the contribution you want to make? How do you want to be spending your time? What skills do you want to develop and have time for more of, and how do you want to develop your people? Make decisions based on that, being intentional rather than just what's in front of you, and what needs to be done and what needs to be done perfectly.

In sum, you want to use the idea of Be Objective to have awareness about where your perfectionism is helpful, and where harmful.

POINTS TO REMEMBER

- Distinguish where your perfectionism is helpful – "healthy striving" and where it is harmful.
- Take Imperfect Action
- Perfectionism creates a stress response which has 3 components. You can lift off the perfection cycle by Balancing your "On" and "Off" button and creating time for Off button/reflective thinking
- Shift from the question "Is it/Am I perfect?" to What's the Purpose of my project?

NEXT STEPS

- Chapter 4 of Success under Stress book has techniques you can do in 1-3 minutes that press that "Off" button during busy days so you can access the part of your brain for reflective thinking and be less reactive. Chapter 5 has techniques to create more uninterrupted time for reflective thinking to get you out of the details and thinking more strategically about your business and life. Pick up a copy of Success under Stress online at Amazon or at your local bookstore.
- You can practice the brief breathing techniques I refer to by having me count it out for you. Download the audio at **www.sharonmelnick.com/mentalreset** or look through the program that teaches the whole Success under Stress toolkit at www.sharonmelnick.com/sus.
- You can download some of the exercises in this chapter at **www.doubtfreenow.com**

Chapter 10:
From Self-Doubt to Self-Trust:
How to Live up to Your Potential

I'm confident in who I am. I've come to a place in my life where I've accepted things that are me, as opposed to feeling pressure to explain myself to people around me. That's just the way I've always tried to be.

– Lady Gaga, Award Winning Singer and Activist

As you shift your attention away from being reassured by what other people think, you might feel adrift in the ocean without an anchor. "But how will I know if I'm doing ok if I can't seek validation from others? How can I trust myself? Is it fear or is it intuitive perception of a red flag?"

In this chapter, I will share how you can trust your most highly prized resource – your own intuition. When you trust your own intuition, it will reduce the angst of making decision. You'll shave off all the time you spin your wheels trying to figure out what to do. You'll know how to act in the heat of the moment.

This strategy is an offspring of the idea, Be Objective. Most people are vague about their doubts and whether they should trust their own judgment. Decisions about whether to speak up, whether to go for it are made through a subjective filter of how you are feeling about yourself in that moment. Do I know enough? Should I do this? But we've come too far; you now know too much! You know you want to shift from subjective to objective. Let's borrow from that cultural low point Olivia Newton-John song from the early 1980's ("Let's Get Physical") – and say, 'Let's get Empirical!' Don't leave it up to your opinion in the moments that count.

As discussed in Chapter 7, it's easier to tackle a demon you can define. So, use this four-column exercise to help you build an empirical database of whether to trust your judgment – and how to improve it if you can't. You are going to log your intuitions and see if, over time, your intuitions/judgment have merit and should be trusted, or whether you want to hone your intuition meter more. Here's how to use the Intuition Log (See Diagram 11):

In Column 1, record just a few words about the situation.

In Column 2, record what your intuition or judgment is.

In Column 3, record what you did about it. Did you follow your judgment? Did you speak up, did you make the call, etc.? Or did you see a problem coming down the pike but *didn't* speak up about it?

In Column 4, record the outcome. [Note: you may not be able to fill it out at the time; record it once you have indication about the outcome.] Did you recommend an action and it had a good outcome? Did your decision lead to a good result? Were your ideas well-received; was it a good strategic recommendation? Did your inhibition turn out to be for good cause? Did the problem you *didn't* speak up about blow up and you could have prevented it?

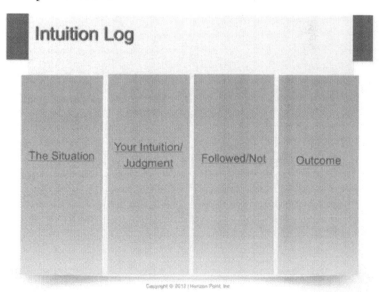

Diagram 11

Keep this log over the course of 1 to 6 months and periodically review it. You want to look for the pattern of what you did and what the outcome was. If you see it's a high percentage of times you followed your intuition with a good outcome (let's say 8 or 9 out of 10x), then there is strong empirical justification for you to trust yourself. In the moment when you are questioning yourself, you can now take it out of your opinion and make a statement of fact that you should trust your judgment. For the 1-2 times that you were off base in your actions, it's helpful to do an 'after action review' and figure out why. Did you listen to the advice of the last person you talked to without trusting your own judgment? Did you overlook cues you could have seen or that you did see but overrode? You also want to note if your hit rate of a desired outcome is relatively low. Then this is an "Accomplish" strategy (from Chapter 7) and you want to take steps to develop your judgment and critical thinking.

Use this Intuition Log as a tool wherever you are under pressure to make a decision, especially in the face of ambiguity or not enough information. It will help you keep your own counsel and trust your gut. And remember that the book *Blink* by Malcolm Gladwell also showed many examples of when it's important to not trust one's judgments, so this strategy will combine keeping your own counsel with a "Be Objective" strategy.

You can also use related critical thinking strategies. For example, maybe take the pressure off to make a decision on the whole situation. Can you identify a smaller piece on which you do have enough information to move forward with now and make a plan to get the rest of the information? Even just distinguishing what you have to make a decision on *now* and what you don't is furthering the work. Finally, making time for that Off button thinking will help connect the dots and connect you with your intuition (see Chapter 7 and my *Success under Stress* book)

POINTS TO REMEMBER

- Your self-talk about whether you can 'trust' your judgment is subjective; make it objective.
- Use the exercise of an Intuition Log to build an empirical database and look for a pattern that tells you whether justified to trust your intuition, or not.

NEXT STEPS

- Download your own copy of your Intuition Log at **www.doubtfreenow.com**
- Leave your comments about the Confidence when it Counts book at **www.facebook.com/groups/confidencecounts**
- **www.Vervago.com** is an excellent resource for developing your critical thinking.

Chapter 11:
From Approval Seeking to Accomplished:
How to Get "Emotional Oxygen" and Validation
from Within
(While Making a Bigger Contribution)

"Sisters are doin' it for ourselves!"

- Eurythmics song, lead singer Annie Lennox, 1985

"I just had an 'aha' moment" a leader blurted out as I was giving a training for her and her high potential women colleagues. "I pride myself on emailing people back immediately. It makes me feel like they know I'm smart and responsive. Instead, I should use my time to think strategically and get back to people during designated blocks for email." Lena Dunham, actress and creator of the hit television show, *Girls*, echoed the temptation of this leadership trainee: "A compliment like 'you're the fastest emailer I know,' or 'how do you do so much at once?' was better than a romantic sweet nothing to me. It fulfilled my desire to be seen as unsinkable, reliable. And in the deepest place, lovable [My business partner] reminded me that meeting a deadline wasn't the reason I was loved or not loved, respected or not respected, and that life didn't have to be an endless jog to accommodate all the Yes's."[vii]

Recognize these descriptions of Indirect path behaviors? In this chapter, you will learn how to stop getting your validation through other people, and instead get it through your own means. I want to show you that Go Direct is the only reliable way to feel rewards in a deep and sustaining way for your life. And not only that, but the rewards are bigger and better! This chapter is especially for you if you are a

Performer or a Perfectionist, but it's relevant for anyone who ever works hard to get others' validation or to live up to their expectations.

If I asked you to identify what would feel really good for you – what would make you feel truly filled up – if you answered honestly, you might say "for my boss to recognize me" or a similar request for a parent/business partner/client to, in some way, 'make you feel' good. It seems like all you want is to just finally have that feeling of worthiness, so you can exhale and believe it. If you have been giving selflessly to others for a long time, you deserve that and it's long overdue. But just as we discussed in regard to formulating your Horizon Point, we no longer want to have an intention 'to be respected,' 'to be acknowledged' because we can't control others' behavior. Instead of an intention to 'get love,' you want to bring the power back within and set an intention to 'be loveable'. From 'respected' to 'worthy of respect'. Because THAT you CAN control!

Before we go over strategies to get that validation from within, let me take a brief digression and put on my professorial hat. *Why do highly capable adult women care so much about what other people think and still feel the need to exceed every expectation?* It started out as our normal way of getting our "emotional oxygen". When growing up we need to breathe physical oxygen to nourish our cells, and we need emotional oxygen to grow our esteem. We are wired to seek that physical and emotional safety, comfort, and feedback from caregivers. We come to know ourselves through the eyes of others. It's the way we know how to feel good and deserving in ourselves, and know where the boundary between others ends and ours begins. Children in families where there are people capable of loving a child 'just for being you' develop this inner worthiness naturally. Such caregivers are contingently responsive to a child's needs and from this repeated interaction pattern over the early years, a child comes to learn she is 'loveable' and deserving of being reasonably taken care of.

When a child doesn't receive that contingent responsiveness, she has to develop ways of getting it – because it's oxygen and we need it to survive. Our Indirect behaviors are an adaptation, developed as a strategy to fulfill our basic emotional oxygen needs – love, attention, encouragement, appreciation, and feeling valued, recognized, worthy, etc. Although children have a variety of adaptations available to them and sometimes choose one that is gender-incongruent (e.g., some girls become bullies), girls are shaped toward a 'caregiving' adaptation more often than boys because it aligns with their socialization.

This aspect of 'pleasing' is a continuation of approaches that have worked to get one's emotional oxygen to date. As we transition to becoming an adult, the maturational path is to shift from getting our needs fulfilled by others, to fulfilling them with peers, and then fulfilling them for others (once in a parent/mentee/caregiving role) where we provide emotional oxygen to others. This chapter shows you how to be intentional about making this shift and feeling fulfilled in yourself. It's great to get a compliment – and I want you to receive many of them – but you can only take it in when, within yourself, you already feel loveable and deserving of that compliment.

Here are 5 ways you can get your emotional oxygen and validation from within. Notice that by putting your time, energy, and attention into these independent forms of fulfillment, you will shift from a 'small game' to a 'bigger game' for your life.

1. Act in the service of your Horizon Point.

This is the 'do it yourself' version. Decide who you want to be (aka, Your Horizon Point) and then 'become her' (see Chapter 5 for a refresher on your Horizon Point) – do not try to get someone else to make you feel that way.

Many of the headaches you have in relationships come from trying to get this validation through others. This idea is summarized in a quote from the comedian Whitney Cummings: "When my therapist first suggested that I was codependent, I was confounded because I wasn't dating anyone. I thought it meant you were in a bad relationship with someone else, when it really means you're in a bad relationship with yourself."[viii]

Don't see your ability to have the inner experience you want to have as being contingent on anyone else's behavior. You can embody who you want to be and how you want to feel at any given moment, simply by setting your intention on it and doing the exercises at the end of Chapter 5.

2. Distinguish 'good hope' from 'bad hope.'

Indirect behaviors that attempt to gain others' validation are a giant vacuum sucking away your time and energy. Though many of us intuitively know this to be true, we don't know how to get off the treadmill. That's because we are 'looking for love in all the wrong places.'

The psychological mechanism of this approval seeking Indirect Behavior is Hope. Your indirect behaviors performed in the hope that 'your middleman' (the person you are hoping to get validation from) will give you the compliments and appreciation you seek. As encouraged in the exercise at the end of the Chapter 4 on Go Direct: When you are tempted to do an approval-seeking behavior, instead, play out the scenario in your mind the way it has historically gone. Sometimes the person comes through for you and compliments you in a satisfying way – when it does, you want to make sure you really take it in and not shrug it off because it was hard won. But more often than not, the person's response will be disappointing at best, and traumatic at worst. As you start to have an awareness of your Indirect path behaviors, you'll likely have a feeling in the pit in your stomach – recognition that it probably won't work out the way you hope and maybe it's time to stop 'looking, and waiting, and hoping, and trying.' That's a moment when confidence counts; a moment in which 'two roads diverged in a single wood' and you can make a powerful choice to Go Direct.

For example, I have a girlfriend who was having trouble ending an unhappy relationship. Despite months of experiences in which her boyfriend was self-absorbed, using her for money, and giving mixed messages about a future together, she kept fighting to keep the relationship alive. In those situations, you feel angry and hurt by the other person's behavior – alternating between "can't they see how worthy I am? and "maybe I'm not as worthy as I hoped I was." Even still, your attention is going toward trying to understand THEIR behavior and hoping you'll finally figure out the one thing you could do to change it.

This is the Indirect path, weighing their opinion/behavior of you more than your own or than is objectively true. What will enable you to get their hooks out of you? Reframe the situation. Stop seeing the relationship as being about what they are doing or not doing, but rather see what *you* are contributing to the situation. Face squarely the fact that you're staying in it out of HOPE. That takes you out of a situation you can't control and puts you back in the driver's seat. It can be painful but this is a situation in which ripping off the band aid can be helpful.

Sometimes, you are hanging in the situation because of your 'Lead Story' about yourself. You think that you can only achieve your goals or feel worthy in yourself through or because of the other person. That's why it is hard to disconnect and you keep coming back for more. Because the alternative feels like giving up on your dreams or admitting that you were not worthy enough. Neither of which is true.

The only thing that is true is that you disconnected from yourself somewhere along the way and handed over your power on a silver platter to the other person. Even if that person has achieved more than you at this point, that person has many times revealed that they are limited and not capable of the meaningful connections you are. Tell an alternative story, a new story: "If they don't see your worth, it's because they are not capable of seeing it."

So, let them go and come home to you. Know that if you are hanging on to something, it's because on some level it has already been lost. And for good reason – because it's not giving you what you need. In the next two points, we'll go over how to get what you want and need – in spades and on demand – first in your work life and then through your self-care.

3. Get your rewards from your contribution.

In this chapter, I am encouraging you to think about where and how you get your rewards, the sense of value, belonging, connection, enjoyment, and meaning for your life. Indirect path behaviors try to get these 'goodies' from other people's compliments and reassurance. When you have meaningful connections in equal, safe, communicative, two-way relationships, the rewards of these meaningful connections can make 'life worth living.' When your approaches are Indirect, you 'give to get'– and if you do so with people who may be limited at giving them to you, the 'goodies' feel like crumbs and fail to satisfy. If stuck in those situations, it's best to find independent ways of getting your rewards or find a way out.

Go back to you. Find your sense of purpose, remind yourself of YOUR goals, and re-connect with the contribution you've been put here to make. Then go after that contribution and actually enjoy the ride. Get your name associated with a big win and it will be on your track record forever. When you accomplish something from your own efforts, no one can ever take that away from you. Put your time, energy, and attention into switching from getting your rewards through others to getting rewards from your contribution. Notice how this approach gives a quantum leap increase to your contribution, bringing you ever more rewards.

One of my clients had responsibility for launching and operating a European business in a Latin American country (it was small relative to the rest of the global business.) A "Performer" and "Perfectionist/Criticizer" by Confidence Type, she demanded that her team met deadlines and drove them to show results in the new business. She was frustrated and resentful that she didn't feel more valued.

In our coaching, she learned to Go Direct! She started to put less effort into getting recognized for her (many) contributions, and more into enjoying her role, freeing herself up from the day-to-day tactics to think more strategically. She increasingly empowered her team members and their performance became closer to her expectations. As the leader of the business, she hit a crossroad at a benchmark period of time; despite a lot of hard work, they were not gaining desired traction in the business. In the past, she would have worked her team harder and shown displeasure with their 'not good enough' results. With her new mindset of Go Direct, she reviewed the entire landscape and decided that it would be more fruitful to put resources into another part of the world. How did she make that decision? Her analysis revealed a lack of fit between their product and the country's culture – that's being Objective! But also, she was less focused on 'getting results that would lead to her recognition' and was more focused on being a strategic leader with an enterprise-wide mentality. From this "Horizon Point," she made the right business decision. And was praised for her strategic thinking and given equally interesting new opportunities.

4. Feel good in your body.

There are certain conditions under which your body feels expansive and calm. In this state, you naturally feel more alive and happy. You might literally feel 'filled up' with oxygen from deeper breaths. Think I'm referring to an illicit drug? Think again. You already have the tools within to achieve this bliss, on demand.

To deal with daily demands, your body has an "On" button – which gives you energy to focus and solve problems - and an "Off" button – which offers you calm and rejuvenation. We are supposed to have balance between the On and Off buttons but the way we live today, we are "always On" and see it as too indulgent to press the Off button. Being able to 'press the Off button' during crazy, demand filled days gives you instant access to autonomous ways of feeling good. (**For the full toolkit how to do this, see my first book, Success under Stress or online training www.sharonmelnick.com/sus**).

The obligations of daily living – piled on by our Indirect path behaviors – wear us thin. And putting our supply line to the 'feel goods' in the hands of other people makes us feel out of control. What's the effect and what's the quickest way forward from it?

Here is an excerpt of my interview with Marcelle Pick, OB/GYN NP and pioneer in women's health who's worked with dozens of thousands of women in her practice. She gives some background and tips on getting back to an energetic feeling and recovering from stress on your body:

"If I'm trying to do everything, and do it perfectly, and always running late to things, this affects us not only physically but also genetically, it can change gene expression. I don't think I see any woman in my classes that does not feel, on a scale of 1 to 10, pretty low in regards to their body. They're too fat, they're too skinny, they're too tall, they're too small, they're not the right size. I'm blown away at how often I see that. Any kind of self-deprecation or self-talk is affecting their cortisol level.

For example, women have PMS because of a low progesterone issue. Biochemically, there is a hormone called pregnenolone, and it makes progesterone. If somebody has a lot of stress for a long period of time and they're self-punishing, they are perfectionists, and they don't like their body, or the culture's telling them they're not enough or not good enough or smart enough in a culture that is dominated by men, all those things are going on. Instead of the pregnenolone making progesterone, it makes cortisol (the stress hormone). This makes estrogen dominance and that has health consequences.

First, stop processed foods. When you change the food, it changes everything. It changes the neurotransmitters, it changes serotonin, and it changes energy level, it changes mitochondria production, it changes the whole physiology. Start to cut out sugar first. (People that crave sugar usually have low serotonin levels, when I correct that they are not as depressed.) Then, I'll have them be more mindful of carbohydrates. Breakfast should not be a meal that you start with carbs. Because the body has been fasting over night for 12 hours. You don't want to start the day with a carb load. What you do is you start the day with protein: A whey smoothie, or some kind of bean smoothie, some kind of rice smoothie, or eggs. I tend to get people off gluten as well. Gluten tends to be extremely problematic for many people in this country. I'll have them sit down and eat breakfast peacefully. Then, I add a multi vitamin and fish oil.

Next, we start to put exercise back into their day. Just changing their diet, getting the sugar and the junk out of their diet, and exercising when they say they want to often gives women the sense of control that they haven't had. When they start to feel that, and that's back to biochemistry just a little bit more stable and the blood sugars are a little bit more stable. Once they do that they start to have a little bit of that energy back. And then they can take on some of the emotional work."

(For extremely helpful information on women's hormones and natural remedies for being healthy and having positive brain chemistry in the pre- and menopausal years visit:

www.MarcellePick.com, www.saragottfriedmd.com, www.drkellyann.com, www.drritamarie.com, www.drbrighten.com, www.jjvirgin.com, www.cassmd.com)

Reinforcing what Marcelle Pick said: starting to make small changes in what you eat and getting regular exercise can result in big changes in how you feel. It can start to make YOU feel back in control again. One of my clients recently said to me, "it was when I started to take time for myself that all the things we talked about really came alive. That's when I started to feel 'in my bones' that I was valuable and it started to become second nature to act that way at work."

There are many ways to access states of calm and expansiveness within yourself, and I highly recommend all of them. Making the time and doing the planning for this derive from your own sense of deserving and from your being proactive about Go Direct ways of getting that good feeling from within:

- Meditation
- Yoga
- Outdoors and Nature
- Exercise
- Beauty (being in the presence of beautiful things and places and really taking it in)
- Candles as part of your pre-sleep ritual
- Baths
- Massages
- Flowers

It's about making time for yourself to practice and experience them. You'll have to be proactive because the world won't part the waters and make time for you. What is your plan to regularly 'make a date with YOURSELF' to access the vast reserve of calm within?

5. Get more from your current relationships.

This is the 'acres of diamonds' strategy, referring to the parable in which a man travels the world seeking diamonds when they were already in the backyard of the farm he sold out of despair that he was poor. You already have relationships; why not take the opportunity to receive and feel even more filled by them? Always harkening back to the idea of "Be Impeccable for your 50%" from my first book, Success under Stress, what is within your control to feel like you are getting even more from your current relationships? You already have relationships – at work, at home, with your family of origin, in your community. Are you doing what you can to make those relationships feel mutual and fulfilling? Are you open and honest? Do you ask for what you need (and, in personal relationships, do so playfully or flirtatiously) or do you resent others for not reading your mind? Do you bring your concerns to the other person with gentle requests or with criticism that shuts them down? Do you make quality time to nurture the closeness?

A great way to get more of what you need from relationships is to know your specific 'love language' and that of people you frequently interact with. This refers to the specific ways you best take in your 'emotional oxygen' (To assess yours' and others', turn to the books on *The 5 Love Languages in Personal and Professional Relationships* by Gary Chapman.)

Here's an example of how to get more out of business relationships. My client was part of an active networking group and was one of the people who gave out the most referrals to others. She was beloved in the group! Problem was that she received only a trickle of referrals back and started feeling resentful. Rather than let it fester, we scripted out how to ask for what she wanted (without coming across as being too 'pushy' to avoid the common bias against women.) As is often the case, the leadership of the group was not tracking this discrepancy, and was very concerned. Note that she maintained a neutral story and didn't get stuck on seeing them as 'lazy' or 'selfish.' The leadership hopped to reminding the members of her desired clients. Let's just say this revved up her referrals and revenue! (And if you ask effectively but others don't respond, it may be time to reevaluate whether those are the right people to be in your life.)

You also want to take a look at how you are responding to other's expectations. Lena Dunham realized that:

"the expectations I was running so hard to meet were expectations I had myself created. It was a slow process, but a polite "no" soon entered my vernacular. "I can't do it realistically by Friday," or "I wish I could be on that panel but my week is insane," or even "no, I'm not comfortable with this dynamic." And something miraculous happened: my personal life followed suit. I can't be at the birthday party. I don't want to go to laser tag ever as long as I live. I am exhausted. People respond well to honesty, to reality. They understand.

You can see her struggle with setting boundaries, but she finally 'owned her value.' That means she realized she could have the energy and focus to accomplish so much more of what she is here for by being intentional about her time and efforts. What could you do if you could be freed up to focus on it? What could you do if you felt supported in your day to day? You want to make decisions and interact with people from the vantage point as if you are already that accomplished person you want to be.

Here is an exercise you can do to help you figure out the boundaries of where you want to say yes, and where you want to say no. We are going to borrow the idea of making an investment and wanting to see ROI (a return on your investment); that means, you want to maximize your emotional oxygen and the rewards you experience in your life. The investment isn't money, it's your time, energy, and attention on a daily basis. It's your 60,000 thoughts a day.

I am now officially making you the Portfolio Fund Manager of YOUR life. Let's look at what you have been investing your time, energy, and attention in – and see if we can increase your ROI!

First, decide on the experience you want to have in your life (then we can decide if your current energy commitments are helping you get there). So, make a list of what you WANT to experience as much as possible in your life (e.g., Contribution, Financial security, Freedom, Connection, Self-Expression, etc., etc.)

_____

_____

_____

Next, list the investments you currently have in your portfolio. These are the activities and relationships that you are devoting your time, energy, and attention to: work, a romantic relationship, child relationships, community work, self-care/exercise, etc.

Third, give a rating how well each of these major 'investments' is doing at giving you the experiences you WANT. For each 'holding,' make a decision about where it fits in your life/portfolio. For holdings that give you high ROI, keep them and spend even more time there if you can. For holdings that drain you, what could you do to raise the value of that stock? For example, your relationship with your boss and team at work will probably be a major holding. What could you do to get more of what you want from that/those relationships? Bring more awareness and intention to the way you are operating in the different areas of your life. You are the Portfolio Manager after all! You have the ability to buy, hold or sell! (I've had people in my programs "sell" the holding of their mother-in-law ;-) and "buy" more time on self-care/exercise or volunteer activities, etc.

Do this exercise as a fun way to plan out a life in which you are intentionally say Yes or No. And then you too can have as Lena Dunham says in the final sentence of her above quote: "From those no's, YES sprung back up everywhere. Funny how that works."

POINTS TO REMEMBER

- Act in the service of your Horizon Point.
- Discontinue hope that others who are limited can give you what you need.
- Increase your contribution and you will experience increased sense of satisfaction.
- Regularly engage in practices that make you feel expansive in your body; engage in dietary practices and exercise make you feel in control.
- Do your part to invigorate your current relationships to feel more fulfilled by them.
- Be the "Portfolio Fund Manager" of your Life. Be intentional about you how you invest your time, energy, and attention and seek the greatest return on your investment

NEXT STEPS

- Trying to figure out where to set your boundaries and say no vs yes? Download the "Portfolio Exercise"
  www.doubtfreenow.com
- Share your insights and commitments to get your 'emotional oxygen' and validation from within, join the Facebook group of smart readers like you at
  www.facebook.com/groups/confidencecounts

Chapter 12:
From Pigeon-Holed to Promoted:
How to Break Out of the Box and Get Promoted

To play a bigger game you must be a bigger you. How can you use the ideas in this book to make a bigger impact? Let's get this party started! (Be in touch and let me know your successes at www.facebook.com/groups/confidencecounts/

However, many smart, capable women who earn glowing performance reviews feel stuck. You are not advancing on the timeline you expected. You feel under-recognized, under-utilized, and unfulfilled. You've overstayed in your role and feel you could contribute so much more than you are.

You feel you have been put in a box, pigeon-holed.

To get to your next level and make your mark you usually have to break out of the box you have been put in.

The first step is to change your own perception of yourself. *The first sale is always to yourself.* Do YOU see yourself as a senior executive, a million-dollar business owner, or a community leader? All the strategies in this book point you toward believing in yourself.

The next step in breaking out of that box is to get others to see you that way too – whether it's a senior leader who is in a position to promote you or someone who could hire or fund you.

When you don't feel recognized, or are not advancing in the way you want, you no longer feel your desired career path is in your control. When you've been waiting, hoping, and trying unsuccessfully to get your manager or another decision maker to recognize you and advance you, it makes you feel powerless. It's reminiscent of the feelings in the Indirect approach.

And it's confusing. You don't know what is holding you back from being offered greater responsibility.

You might question *yourself*: What should I be doing differently? Is there a perception about me that is holding me back? You might even question whether you are in the right field or whether you have what it takes.

It's common to feel like the organization controls your career and your future. Your language might even reflect this way of thinking, such as:

"I was told…"

"The company is going through a restructuring; it's best to wait it out…"

"I have to wait until my boss retires…"

You *know* – intellectually – that you have choices, but it doesn't *feel* that way.

Your energy drains. You feel trapped.

It doesn't have to be like this. It doesn't have to be up to the organization as to when you get promoted – it can be up to YOU. You can get promoted on YOUR OWN timeline, without having to wait until the dust settles, without having to wait for your boss to retire, without having to wait to bring it up again at next year's performance review.

If others have put you in a box, here is my 'no-fail' strategy to break out of that box and get promoted. It's a strategy to take back the control so you can act more powerfully and change perceptions of those in a position to promote you.

The idea is to declare and pursue a BOLD GOAL.

A Bold Goal is a specific result or outcome that enables you to add greater value to the organization. The pursuit of this outcome requires you to rise above your day-to-day responsibilities and showcases your strategic and leadership capabilities. It makes you visible to a broader group of stakeholders – especially those who are more senior to you or occupy decision-making roles – so they can get to know you and create a new perception of you as someone who is 'ready' for the next level. If you have been in your role too long and feel bored or unfulfilled, your Bold Goal should re-energize your passion and position you for future opportunities.

Perhaps your ultimate outcome is to get promoted or become involved in more interesting, strategic projects. If so, great! Now ask yourself: What perception of you must the decision maker have in order to envision you in that next-level role?

The Bold Goal is a value-added initiative/project/presentation you do to help you create that perception. **In keeping with the idea of Go Direct, it's a way to make the first move – to do something that proactively changes others' perception of you.** It's something you take on to further your ultimate outcome.

If you need to be seen as more strategic, then pursue a Bold Goal that showcases your ability to be strategic. Perhaps take the lead to convene a committee that fixes a cross-functional problem. Maybe lead a review of your data practices and make recommendations.

If you need to be seen as more of a leader, take the lead on an initiative – even if it's a volunteer opportunity or a way of stepping up to lead within your own function.

Even better is to have your Bold Goal accomplish something that benefits a lot of people, thus causing a ripple effect where people know about and follow you. Examples of this kind of Bold Goal might be to win a certain big account, or get buy-in for a major change you recommend within your organization, or convene a conference that is well respected.

Want to be inspired as you are formulating your own Bold Goal? Here's a story of Emily whose Bold Goal got her promoted in just 60 days.

In sales at a pharmaceutical company, Emily did a great job each day and got terrific reviews. She could have continued with this role and stayed 'in her box', but she knew she wanted MORE. She wanted to advance and assume more interesting responsibilities. Yet she felt stuck; her efforts to expand her role hadn't been supported.

Emily enrolled in my Confident Influential Leader: *Get Heard, Get a Next Role* virtual coaching program. Whereas in the past she would have waited for someone else to initiate conversations around her idea, this program trains participants on how to declare and achieve a Bold Goal within 90 days and get promoted.

She observed a need for people in the field who felt isolated and didn't always receive up to date information. She translated her intuitions and observations into an action that benefitted multiple stakeholders, making that critical *first move*. In her case her Bold Goal was to bring add value by innovating and organizing an event for people in the field to share best practices and connect with one another.

Pursuing this Bold Goal required her to step up. At first, she felt afraid of putting herself out there to lead this unprecedented initiative, so she had to get over her fear.

In order to get volunteers to help (which was over and above their daily responsibilities) she had to learn to inspire them. (Note: Inspiration is the leadership quality that best catalyzes discretionary effort and productivity from others).

She also had to deal with her perfectionism, and learn how to leverage it for those few aspects of the event that were detail-oriented, but allow others to implement their own ideas as well.

Additionally, she had suggested this Event idea to decision makers before and got a "No", so it took courage to bring it up again. This time she used skills she learned in the coaching program for effective Influence, so she got a "Yes" to her request. She even got the company's corporate executive vice president of sales to speak at the event.

The result? The event was an incredible success. The EVP of sales was so impressed that he declared this kind of event should become a standard and best practice for the company.

He featured her at the national company's town hall meeting. On top of that, she was asked to present on a panel to the company leadership. She was so well received that she was invited to a small private dinner with C-Suite officers at the home of the company's CEO.

Within 60 days she was promoted! The invisible hand of the organization came out and tapped her for greater responsibilities and advancement.

None of this would have happened had she stayed in her 'box,' doing a great job every day, but hadn't chosen to pursue a Bold Goal that required her to step up and get senior leaders she didn't know to become aware and think well of her.

Declaring a Bold Goal and then learning the skills to achieve it is a game-changing approach to your career. It puts YOU in control of your career path.

Once you declare a Bold Goal, you want to learn and apply the skills that will help you achieve it.

In the Confident Influential Leader: *Get Heard, Get a Next Role* program, participants learn the skills that support them to achieve their

Bold Goal and raise their game. There is an emphasis on the three essential skillsets that set you up for next level opportunities: **Influence**, **Confidence**, and **Resilience**.

Influence centers on how to get a YES for your requests and buy-in for your ideas. You want to start by making a Stakeholder Map of all the decision makers who touch on the issue you want to impact through your Bold Goal, and identify what advantages each, as well as the organization, will gain from your "Ask." With this information, you can customize your pitch to each stakeholder. This kind of influencing campaign is typically more effective than simply asking for a next-level role just because you want it.

Confidence concerns applying your skills to Go Direct in your own life. Once you are consistently confident, it's important to regularly convey that confidence in your communications. You want to know how to speak up and push back, even when you don't have all the answers. The way to do that is to communicate with authority about both what you do and do not know. (E.g., "We know x, but we don't know y. Here's why it's been a challenge to know y, here's my plan to obtain more data on it, and I'll supply you with a report on this by the end of the week.")

Resilience is about skills to balance the 'busy' tactical part of your brain that pushes you to tick items off your 'to do' list with the ability to access the calm, bigger picture part of your brain. So you can stay present at home and at work, and stay a Calm leader when others are frenetic. This skill is relevant to many women because we are emotionally attuned to care about relationships and how we are seen, and we can often set ourselves up to React. (See also Chapter 8, and Chapters 9/10 in *Success under Stress* for more on this skillset). Also, there is a known gender bias that women are 'emotional,' and in performance reviews that give feedback about these soft-skill issues, 76% of women (versus only 2% of men) receive feedback about this idea of being 'too emotional' or 'not confident'. Staying poised is a counter-bias behavior and changes people's perception to see you even more as a leader.

The skillset of resilience provides you the tools to rise above the tyranny of your 'to do' list and be strategic. It also enables you to stay focused and energized during long days and turn off your thoughts and sleep through the night.

These 3 interlocking skillsets (Confidence, Resilience, Influence) help you pave the path to a next-level role and have more impact. If you see the relevance for your life and career path, I encourage you to learn more about the Confident Influential Leader: *Get Heard, Get Promoted* program and see if it's a good fit to join the next cohort at **www.sharonmelnick.com/cil**.

POINTS TO REMEMBER

- Declare and pursue a Bold Goal – an initiative that takes you out of your day to day responsibilities, showcases your strategic abilities, and enables you to have visibility to senior leaders who don't know you well.
- This approach has a strong track record of getting smart women 'out of their box' and promoted on an accelerated timeline.
- Confidence, Resilience, Influence are interlocking skills that sets women up to be successful leaders

NEXT STEPS

- Ready to expand your responsibility, get promoted, and have more influence in your organization? Be inspired of case studies of other women who have done so and find out the full formula at **www.sharonmelnick.com/cil**.
- Tell us about your Bold Goal at **www.facebook.com/groups/confidencecounts**

Chapter 13:
Is it Me, or Is it Bias?
How to Rise Above Bias and Regain Your
Confidence

This book is about helping you create a confident and objective self-perception, to trust in your abilities, and to fully express your talents. If bias affects others' evaluation of your performance and potential to contribute to the organization, it can contaminate the objectivity of the feedback you receive.

And when you hope for an outcome and see the chances of that outcome diminishing for you, it is frustrating and can erode your confidence.

What's the evidence?

Young women and men enter the workforce with similar levels of confidence, but within two years in the work world the confidence of young women plummets, while that of young men stays the same, or rises (Bain & Company, 2015). According to a survey of 10,000 professionals at the mid-career and senior level, although young men and women enter with similar levels of confidence to reach senior management (27–28%), only 13% of mid-career women and 29% of seasoned career women have this belief, in contrast to 25% and 55% of men, respectively (Bain & Company, 2015). Women's aspiration for senior leadership and confidence in achieving it plummets 50% and 60%, respectively, as they experience the realities of the workplace.

Across levels, the expected representation of women is 15% lower than that of men. In short:

"Women see a workplace skewed in favor of men. They are almost four times more likely than men to think they have fewer opportunities to advance because of

their gender—and are twice as likely to think their gender will make it harder for them to advance in the future." McKinsey & Company (2015)

Even though this book encourages you to create an internal compass and act according to your own Horizon Point, if you work in an organization, there are still unwritten rules about who advances and who doesn't, and how.

Bias is at play in all our interactions. Biases are non-conscious schemas, a legacy from thousands of years of cultural (and perhaps genetic) heritage. These hardwired representations and assumptions developed in order to help humans quickly make evaluations and decisions. They influence how we process information by giving us shortcuts, such as paying attention to information that fits into theories we already hold, or categorizes whether someone fits a stereotype (making us feel safe) or not (making us feel uncomfortable or alerting parts of our brain to be on guard).

Biases are formed outside of conscious awareness and can often conflict with our consciously held values. Many biases are adaptive because they help categorize people and inform responses in the thousands of situations we face each day. But they can also blind us to new information. Bias may be more prevalent in the business environment of the New Normal, where a fast-paced, multi-tasking culture fosters unconscious and reactive decision making and inhibits reflection and checking of one's bias.

Bias can exist from and toward any social group. In-group bias is prevalent, setting people up to view those who are similar to them more positively.

Bias affects decision making about advancement and funding for women and people of color – i.e., decisions that affect diverse talent's ability to make the contribution they are here to make.

Biases can set an expectation of how you, as a woman, should act – they reward or punish according to long-embedded schemas about gender roles, and you may find yourself in a no-win' dynamic in terms of how to act. Others' behavior will unconsciously be guided to affect decisions about your advancement, whether to hire you, or offer you opportunities, whether they see you as a match in a romantic situation, or how to act in a partnership or family relationship with you, and so on.

In short, women's perception that they are at an unfair disadvantage in terms of advancement erodes their confidence.

Common biases that make it hard for women to be fully expressed as leaders

Likability is key to having influence over others and being seen as a good fit for advancement (as well as having positive work relationships which are important for everyone, and especially meaningful to women).

Yet hardworking women who deliver results are *liked less* when they:

- speak up to the same degree as male leaders
- act incongruently with gender stereotypes (When women act agentic and authoritative, as we expect leaders to do, they face a social penalty. Women are liked at about equal rates to men when they act in a participatory fashion.)
- negotiate for resources or salary
- lead with qualities reflecting their competence vs. leading with warmth
- act with "too much" of an interpersonal approach (Women are often given feedback indicating they are 'too aggressive,' or 'too nice,' or 'too emotional', keeping them in a constant state of self-scrutiny and leaving them little wiggle room to develop a signature leadership style that creates followership.)

Many other common biases toward women affect day-to-day evaluations and opportunities for advancement:

- Women are given less credit for their accomplishments
- Women are penalized more heavily for mistakes
- Women are more frequently evaluated based on past performance whereas men are evaluated based on future potential – this sets women up to need to 'prove themselves again' and inhibits the decision maker from envisioning her in the next-level role.

Subjectively, men tend to inflate their performance ratings while women underestimate their performance. Objectively, when work results are evaluated blind to gender, women's work is rated as, if not more, effective than men's.

Though many of us feel progress is not swift enough, and many women's daily lives are impacted by these biases, there is evidence that through the enormous increase in awareness and commitment to gender parity at all levels of business, schemas about gender is improving, and the number of women in leadership positions is increasing in some sectors.

Some mechanisms by which bias affects confidence

1. Lack of role models

'Imposter syndrome' is more likely in environments where there are few people 'who look like you,' because a common conclusion is "I don't belong here," or "I couldn't do that." You don't see yourself reflected in the external environment even though that has nothing to do with your actual abilities. When the U.S. Supreme Court Justice Sonia Sotomayor stepped onto the campus of Princeton University as the first generation to go to college from her financially disadvantaged community in the Bronx she said she felt like she was visiting an alien land and didn't feel "good enough."

2. Indirect patterns

If you have a history of Indirect patterns, you have been 'other-directed', i.e., taking your cues from others' behavior toward you. This means you track others' perceptions of you and incorporate them into how you perceive yourself. If, prior to reading this book, you have practiced Indirect approaches and have not succeeded in changing decision makers' perceptions about you due to bias or their own limitations, you might mistakenly conclude their lack of updated perception is due to your own limited abilities rather than their bias.

3. Attributions

Women are sensitive to the experience of 'nice words, no action'. As humans, we need to explain this discrepancy and understand why it occurs. Research indicates that men attribute failure to external factors (e.g., the test questions weren't similar to the test prep) and success to internal factors (e.g., "I am smart"). In contrast, women attribute lack of progress to internal factors ("I'm not smart enough") and good results to external factors ("I was lucky; people helped me get the role").

Attributions are similar to the stories we tell (see Chapter 8 a refresh). If you don't get a role, or if you are 'man-terrupted' in a meeting, you might get stuck in a 'lead story' and attribute the event to your lack of ability rather than to objective, situation-specific 'alternative' stories.

4. Control

In the face of not having control over a situation, we humans tend to exert control over those aspects we know we can control in order to avoid feelings of powerlessness. When women can't control decisions to advance, they feel confused. *Why isn't it happening?* This scenario frequently leads to questioning oneself: *Is it me? What am I doing wrong?* She might even ask her boss "What am I doing wrong?", focusing manager attention on perceived deficits rather than strengths that justify promotion.

We do this in personal relationships as well. In my "C-school" program, Michelle found herself 'over-giving' (common to a Performer type but which could be characteristic of any of us). She bled a lot of time and energy into supporting her mother, hoping her mother would one day see how helpful and generous she was and finally, explicitly, express her love for Michelle. When she didn't receive the hoped-for love, she would feel unworthy. Yet, even though she wasn't getting what she needed and deserved, she continued to over-give because it was the part of the interaction she could control. Michelle could only detach from this pattern once she discovered her mother's biology and psychology set up limited behavior. And that her mother's lack of loving response wasn't due to Michelle not being lovable, but because her mother wasn't capable of seeing Michelle for the loving person she truly is. That set her free – she went on to start a very successful company and as she reports: 'develop a profound trust in herself."

5. Lack of opportunity

If you lack increasing opportunity to stretch and lead, you might not further develop these capacities, resulting in these essential qualities becoming something you 'don't yet have,' and leading you to question whether you can/will develop those abilities. Lack of opportunity can be overcome by maintaining a Growth mindset, in which you believe in your ability to learn and progress.

6. Underestimation

Women are likely to underestimate their ability and not apply for a next-level role. It's an oft-cited finding that women only apply for roles when they believe they can successfully meet ALL the criteria for the role versus men who apply when they only meet some of the criteria.

7. Undervaluation

The first sale is always to yourself. If women undervalue themselves, that evaluation might project through interaction patterns. Others will match her level of self-assurance when they negotiate salaries, consider hiring her businesses, or make decisions in a marital relationship about the value of one's time.

8. Social threat

Women use empathy to pick up on social cues. Sensing possible disapproval, or loss of respect, status, or likability, can be considered a threat that would prohibit her from acting with her full power or agency.

Is It You, or Is It Bias? How to Know

One of the tenets of the Go Direct approach is to *Be Objective.* We must be objective when it comes to understanding being caught up in the effects of bias.

If you face a frustrating scenario it can be helpful to sort out what aspects of the situation you CAN control – this objective understanding can set you up to problem-solve effectively. My pithy way of restating this approach is for you to determine "Is it me?" vs. "Is it bias"?

You want to be thoughtful and discern which part of this situation has to do with "me," i.e., *your* abilities, *your* approach. (In my experience, there are almost always a few key skills you can improve to make an impact on changing others' perceptions of your abilities. Many of the chapters in this book illustrate the dramatic change you can make in other's perceptions by shifting your own paradigm from Indirect to Go

Direct!)

You also want to identify which part of your challenging scenario has to do with the decision maker's limitations. Though unpleasant to have to deal with a person who thwarts you, once you know their motivations and limitations, you will better see how to Influence and/or work around that person.

And, finally, once you have been as effective as you can be at the above factors, you may conclude that any remaining blocks are possibly due to bias. In these situations, you can personally endeavor to bring objectivity to the situation, and deliver documented information to a trusted steward of the culture, such as an HR or diversity professional for advocacy.

Let's review each one of these three areas in detail:

1. Does your boss or decision maker possess limitations that have little or nothing to do with you?

You want to become adept at seeing situations objectively and telling stories in the service of your Horizon Point. Sometimes the most freeing story and the best antidote to self-criticism is that the other person has limitations that are causing a challenge. For example, if you are not getting clear feedback, it may be that your manager is uncomfortable giving feedback. Or it may be a combination: maybe your manager is uncomfortable or unskilled in giving feedback in conjunction with your having a history of 'showing emotion' in performance reviews, making that person hesitant to share candid feedback.

Alternatively, a manager might not support you because they feel threatened by you.

Or they are being pressured by their boss to direct resources into a different part of the group.

Or the person is narcissistic and self-absorbed and has limited ability to see others clearly enough to provide helpful feedback and direction.

I encourage you not to take on the blame or ascribe bias when there could be an alternative story that matches the fact pattern better. It's not pleasant to have to deal with a manager or funder or partner who is limited, but at least recognizing this means your self-confidence won't take a hit. Then you know to shift into gear to adjust your influence strategies and maybe not put all your eggs in that single relationship basket. (For a refresh, see Chapter 8.)

2. *Might my lack of desired outcome have something to do with "me" – what I'm bringing to the interaction?*

Remember, we always want to control what we CAN control. (See my first book, *Success under Stress,* for extensive skill building on this topic.) My mantra is: **"Be Impeccable for your 50%."** That means take 100% responsibility for all that goes on within your 50%, and be EFFECTIVE at it *before* focusing attention on matters that are not within your control (such as bias).

In particular, we examined three interlocking skillsets in the previous chapter that support women to be effective leaders. These are important to master if you want to make your mark. Approach every situation by asking: "Have I been Impeccable for my 50%" in terms of my Influence, Confidence, and Resilience.

In each work or relationship challenge, do a self-inventory to determine whether you are being as effective as you can be. If not, you might become unnecessarily frustrated with others and miss out on opportunities to improve the situation through your own efforts.

Questions you can ask yourself include:

Confidence

Have I spoken up/asked? Have I asked effectively, influentially?

Am I doing "Indirect" behaviour or am I going "Direct"? For example, *Am I trying to get a response from the other person? Does this feel familiar to other situations in my life? Do I feel powerful (or powerless) in my body when I do the behavior?*

Do I know in my heart I am doing everything I can on my end before becoming frustrated with others?

Resilience

Am I taking care of myself so I can show up as my best?

Am I balancing a tactical to-do list with big-picture strategic thinking?

Am I being reflective instead of being reactive?

Influence

Have I made my request in terms of "What's in it for them?"

Have I been concise and clear in what I say?

Did I build on other's point of view rather than disagreeing with them?

A common frustration expressed by smart women is: *I spoke up. I said something. But I got a non-response. I was told no.* That lack of response can cause a woman to question her confidence. And it sets her up to believe bias might be operating.

In pivotal situations, increased ability to Influence can reduce the Bias effect.

This is why it's important to always **Be Impeccable for your 50%!** and ask, "Is there anything I can to do be more effective?" *before* making any assumptions.

Here is the story of a woman who was able to overcome her boss's limitations and his pattern of likely bias by improving her ability to

Influence.

Tracey is a seasoned sales person at a Fortune 100 company. When she called me, she said her boss systematically excluded her from opportunities, gave leads to young inexperienced male salespeople, and said no to all her requests for resources – for six years! She thought he was clearly biased. She was frustrated, resentful, and worried about securing her financial future.

"Your boss may indeed be biased," I said, "but we don't know for sure until you have used effective approaches to Influence. Try reframing your requests in terms of 'What's in It for Him'. We know that is an effective approach for getting a Yes:"

She hired me to help her. She wanted to have hope but was skeptical about her upcoming meeting with him because he was so narcissistic and only managed up.

I said, "No problem." Why did I say that?

As long as the person you want to influence possesses strong motivation, you can appeal to that motivation. Even if the motivation is to be 'all about them' and they're not interested in you, you can still leverage it to show them how they will get more of what THEY want if they agree to what you want.

We scripted her requests. She articulated how her requests would help him look good in front of his boss, and how granting them would set him up for the next-level role he covets but has not succeeded in getting.

The idea was that he would see her, and her requests, as the solution to his pressures.

A week later she emailed me.

...my Boss meeting went extremely well. I received ALL my Asks plus I added some more due to the flow and got them all. This is the turning point I have been

waiting 6 years for. Thank you!!!

As long as you have x-ray vision into your decision maker's psychology, you can Influence them to go along with your ideas. And ask on behalf of others, it increases the gravitas of your request.

Remember: don't waste your time trying to get someone to recognize you or say yes when they have demonstrated they are not supportive. This is an Indirect approach and all it does is make you feel powerless.

AND don't keep trying to get someone who is limited and upward-focused to spontaneously evolve and be capable of paying more attention to you!

Rather, use a Go Direct approach: Pursue a Bold Goal (Do something that breaks you out of your everyday duties, showcases your strategic abilities, and exposes you to senior leaders who don't know you well.) (See Chapter 12 for a refresh on the idea of your Bold Goal). Do something that illustrates your unique value proposition to your prospect (or to your romantic date). Do something that demonstrates your unique perspective and makes prospects feel you are the one who understands them better than any other salesperson.

When others see how you are creating buzz, that you are a 'woman in motion' and full of confidence, they will experience #FOMO (fear of missing out) if they don't go along with your requests, meet with you, and/or promote you. They will view you with a new or heightened sense of possibility and offer you opportunities they didn't envision for you before.

3. *Is my lack of progress due to bias?*

How to tell if you are facing bias? Here are some signs to look for:

— Decisions are made without objective fact and the facts don't add up. (E.g., "She's not a good fit. We just prefer working with John,")

– Decision makers can't point out specific instances that justify their perceptions. (E.g., "Can you give an example of when I've been...," and the decision maker can't provide one.)

– You feel singled out or excluded.

– The behavior is systematic.

– It feels like something is going on that isn't explicitly articulated.

– Code words are used to keep the bias hidden.

– Decision makers are not amenable to new or disconfirming information.

– You are asked to prove talents that you already have objective record of achieving in order to be seen as "ready."

How can you respond to bias?

1. <u>Be informed by research on Bias:</u> Instead of losing your confidence thinking it's about you, use your knowledge of research on bias to help guide your behavior. Be aware of common scenarios in which bias might be operating and protect against internalizing others' perceptions. Know the research and self-monitor to a degree that feels natural and emotionally intelligent, not paralyzing. Practice having situation-specific versatility in your style, as that denotes good leadership. Demonstrate warmth alongside competence. Keep displaying that warmth as you negotiate. Even though this requires an extra layer of self-monitoring that men don't have to perform (which admittedly can be exhausting and stressful), use the research to your advantage and get into leadership positions – then change the culture!

2. Act Counter-Bias:

Show up as a calm, poised leader. Negotiate on behalf of others and always make requests in terms of 'What's in it for them?' These are proven antidotes to bias, and they represent best practices for all professionals.

You can also inoculate against bias when you speak up. There is some research that suggests if you have something important to say that might confirm a biased perception (e.g., "She's too aggressive"), you can use an approach of Inoculation to decrease the social penalty associated with the behavior. With this approach, you provide a heads-up that you will do a behavior that is knowingly associated with bias, and give people a 'heads up' you will be doing it. For example, this approach allows you to make a strong statement yet do it intentionally to make an impact rather than doing it out of lack self-awareness or playing out a stereotype. It might sound like "I know you might think I am coming across strongly on this point, but I'm using this tone because I feel so concerned that our patients will suffer if we go this route…"

3. Call out the Bias

You don't have to allow bias or be a bystander when you experience it. Here's what you can say and do in those awkward situations:

Request objectivity: Ask for objective and specific feedback. Ask for specific incidents to support the person's evaluation. Stand up for your colleagues and require that specific, objective feedback with knowable sources is provided.

Request accountability: Bias thrives in the absence of accountability. Ask if the person would be willing to review the criteria for the role with you to identify where you meet criteria and where you don't. This requires them to be objective.

Request that protocols be followed: Ask the in-house human resources professionals whether criteria for the role are being applied objectively.

Ask effectively: Do what you can to help your decision maker see you in that role. When you apply for roles or funding/to get the business, discuss not only your past accomplishments but also how they set you up to carry out the next role. Help your decision maker form a picture in their mind of you in the role/getting the business.

Document it: Keep a record of the facts, of what is said and done. (That will be more powerful evidence to an adjudicator, internally or externally, than any inference you make or conclusions you draw.)

Litigate it: If bias is documentable, you can choose to rise above it (see next section) or litigate it.

How can you regain confidence when it's been worn down by bias?

All the Go Direct strategies in this book will help you be more intentional about who you want to be, no matter what others around you say or do. The more you Go Direct, the more you will prevent erosion of confidence due to bias.

Here are some reminders of what you can do to maintain or regain your confidence in the face of bias.

1. **Rise above.** Remind yourself that people aren't engaging in bias on purpose. You, too, respond from centuries of unconscious bias embedded in your thought patterns, even though you may be more aware and intentional than people who have not been educated about these ideas. Assume positive intent. This is an example of practicing the skill in Chapter 8 to tell a different story about why the facts are happening this way. Remember, you always have a choice in terms who you want to show up as. Although you may lack the necessary control to direct how the situation has unfolded to date, you always have the power

to influence how the interaction unfolds from the moment you become involved in it.

Act in the service of your Horizon Point. Figure out what needs to be said in order for the parties to this discussion to make decisions based on objective criteria.

Try to expand your view of the situation. Rather than only looking at the players in your current situation – which can be extremely frustrating – try to see your situation in an overall march to progress. Appreciate the burgeoning awareness and progress society has made in only the last decade or so about this issue. See yourself as a warrior on the front lines of history. Though it may not satisfy when it comes to getting your specific requests right now, know that all of the new Go Direct approaches you do today are your way of making a dent in the universe of the gender parity issue. Enjoy playing a role for current and future generations. Think of your offspring and mentees, and how you can make it better for them.

2. **Change the paradigm**. If you see that bias is operating in decisions that affect you and people you care about, work to change the system in your organization. Bring your paradigm-changing ideas to leadership and get company influencers onboard. Become involved in your company's women's leadership network or a professional association in your field that is working to create gender parity. Become part of a diversity council in your organization. Raise the issue in meetings (see previous section) and hold colleagues accountable for decisions. If you are a business owner, get certified as a diverse supplier (www.wbenc.org, www.nglcc.org, www.nmsdc.org) and become part of a movement of business owners creating more opportunity and wealth.

Turn your "missing out" into a mission. Run for local, state, or national office. Become part of an advocacy organization. Put your money where your mouth is and become a donor to or volunteer at an organization that reflects the change you want to see in the world.

3. Don't internalize it. Educate yourself about bias so you can recognize when it is at play and not take it personally.

4. Block your susceptibility. Know that an Indirect approach will make you more susceptible. Having self-doubt or criticism is like kindling, which can ignite when sparked by other people's bad behavior and bias.

As we've discussed throughout this book, it is normal, and common, to grow up with an "Indirect" pattern – many of us do. Also, you might have something in your history that makes you susceptible to an Indirect path pattern and internalizing bias. For example, I had a client who grew up in a West Indian family where there was a lot of emphasis on "What will the neighbors think?" That's Indirect. Be aware of it and don't go there.

Although we are all susceptible to bias, you are even more susceptible when your interactions are Indirect and reflect an "other" orientation, where you weigh others' input more heavily than your own and are likely to read into the implications of situations in order to know how YOU are doing.

5. Change your "story." Catch yourself if you explain bias with attributions about your perceived weaknesses. Always look for alternative stories, and tell a different story in the service of your Horizon Point! Consider how your thwarted outcome or experience of micro-aggressions might be caused by reasons other than you're not being worthy of respect. For example, always consider whether or not the situation reflects the decision maker's own limitations. If so, it's not pleasant, but it presents a different barrier than you're not being "good enough," and one that can be overcome with effective strategies for

Influence. (See **www.sharonmelnick.com/cil** for effective Influence strategies so you can change decision makers' perceptions of you.)

6. **Be Objective**. Use the strategies in Chapter 7 to shift from subjective views of yourself that would be more permeable to other people's points of view, and internalizing bias, and instead practice being objective. Base your evaluation and feeling about yourself on objective facts. Focus on future opportunities rather than dwell on the past.

7. **Crush it anyway**! Pour yourself into your End User (see chapter 6 for a refresh) and get results for your clients and your company that are so rewarding you feel in a positive flow. Celebrate those wins. Help others to know about them (the best counter-bias way for women to do this is to have others brag on your behalf). Have so much passion and purpose for the contribution you want to make that you are Teflon to anyone else's biases!

8. **Trust your intuition**. Learn to trust your own intuition and keep your own counsel. (See chapter 11 for a refresh). If you get a bad feeling from the people or the culture, discern whether you can trust your intuition. If so, consider going elsewhere.

9. **Healthy detachment.** When you find yourself in an uncomfortable situation, healthy detachment is a strategy that can get you through until conditions improve. In this strategy, you draw a line in the sand: you describe at what point conditions would become so intolerable that you would take action to avoid being subjected to them anymore, where you would pursue some action to change your circumstances. Any conditions that exist which might be unpleasant or uncomfortable to deal with but don't cross that line you can say "I CHOOSE to stay in this situation because it serves ME and what I WANT." Use the tools in this book and take a Go Direct approach so you can get more of what you want and be the person you want to be while you give the behaviors of decision makers an opportunity to

evolve.

10. **Exercise your options.** Remember that you are not tied or locked in to ANY situation. If you've drawn your line in the sand (as suggested in point no. 9) and that line has been crossed, feel justified and empowered to make a different choice. You can leave or remove yourself from any team, employer, business partnership, or personal relationship – it's YOUR choice of what you want for your life. They don't deserve you. Go where you are wanted!

Be inspired by this empowered lawyer who did just that: *A vivacious lawyer was a partner in a prestigious NY firm but experienced chronic frustration when trying to influence the management. Up against the usual suspects of bias when it came to salary, resources, and a culture of equality, she felt worn down and asked me to help her influence more effectively. Before we could even get started, her years of being a go-to expert paid off: a deep-pocket client engaged her for a very large case, one that promised to keep a lot of lawyers busy for months, and she was the lead on it. It makes me smile just to think of it, because she walked the new client right over to the other top firm down the street, which was known for a culture of equality (and even has a woman whose name is on the door and several women partners leading practices). Go Direct, case closed!*

Follow the advice rendered by Gertrude Stein in one of my favorite quotes: *"The best revenge is a successful life!"*

For Further Reference:

To explore the topic of bias further, please refer to the following resources, referenced in this chapter

2013 Living Progress Report, Hewlett Packard, 2013

Are People Becoming More Open to Female Leaders? Khazan, Olga, <u>The Atlantic,</u> May 2, 2014

Everyday Moments of Truth, Bain and Company, 2015

For Women Leaders, Likability and Success Hardly Go Hand-In-Hand, Cooper, Marianne, <u>Harvard Business Review,</u> April 30, 2013

Knowing When to Ask: The Cost of Leaning In, Exley, Christine L, Niederle, Muriel, Vesterlund, Lise, National Bureau of Economic Research, NBER Working Paper No 22961, Issued December 2016

What Works for Women at Work: Four Patterns Working Women Need to Know, Williams, Joan C and Dempsey, Rachel University Press, 2014

Why Failure Hits Girls So Hard, Simmons, Rachel, <u>Time</u>, August 25, 2015

Why Women' Don't Negotiate Their Job Offers, Bowles, Hannah Riley, <u>Harvard Business Review, June 19, 2014</u>

Women in the Workplace, McKinsey & Company, 2015

Chapter 14:
Be Good in You

You now have a toolkit – practical tools you can use in everyday situations to have Confidence when it Counts. It's been my aim to help you remove what I call "your private suffering" and channel your energies toward the contribution you've been put here to make – in your business, on your team, in your family, in your community, in the world. To be able to rise above the personalized concerns of your draining self talk and act to uplift all involved in the situation. To free up some of the time, energy, and attention involving others in the confidence you can now source from within, and direct it toward your own actualization or toward advocacy for organizational and societal advances in gender parity.

You now know to stop being caught in an Indirect pattern of getting your confidence via managing others' perceptions, and to start on a Go Direct path to worthiness.

You know to orient your days around your new purpose – your intention to act in the service of your Horizon Point.

You know to Be Objective – by deciding on a go-forward solution to your perceived weaknesses. By telling alternative stories instead of stuck in your unexamined gut responses. By having awareness where your Perfectionism is helpful and problem solving around it where harmful. By developing an empirical database to indicate when and why to trust your intuition.

You know to find independent ways of getting validation and your essential 'emotional oxygen'. You can access this supply line to feeling good in you via practices that achieve calm or give you back control over your body. Whether through meditation, yoga, 'power poses', or the presence of natural beauty and art – you know to regularly come home to a connection with yourself. You can shift your attention away from trying to 'get' validation from someone you've been trying to control, and instead get it from a sense of satisfaction with your contributions and deepening the connection with available people in your life.

Through these approaches, you can always be the person who rises above her temptation toward self-doubt and criticism. By rising above, you not only change your own behavior, but you can have a powerful effect to uplift all involved in the situation. Just by showing up authentically as your best self, you can help teams come to better solutions, and help everyone involved in your business to grow.

The more you show up as the calm, confident, influential contributor you want to be, the more you break down the existing bias. When we come up with the best solutions we are the chosen leader. When we are smart about the way we put ourselves out as the 'go to expert' we compel people to hire us. As we earn more, we have more clout over company products and policies.

Though bias has been entrenched in our collective unconscious since the dawn of time, trends are all in a positive direction and with rapid momentum. There are more eyes and ears tracking the issue of gender parity. For example, Gender Avenger is an organization that tracks the degree to which women's voices are represented as speakers and panelists at conferences. The White House recently required transparency in salaries for equal jobs. Men and women are allying in campaigns and projects, such as the He for She campaign. Leaders who display overt bias are terminated.

One of the biggest trends is women taking charge of their destinies and starting their own businesses. The tools to become successful in business and become the 'go to' expert in your field are now democratized – any and every woman with a skill, product, or message can access WordPress website templates, YouTube videos, email marketing, FB ads, or TEDx talks to make her impact.

Another big trend is women helping women, such as women aggregating their investment funds to support women entrepreneurs. "Sisters are doin' it for ourselves"!

The most helpful trend is the one which indicates the seeds of partnership between men and women – and all who have a stake in gender parity (namely, everyone). "Conversations with men", men as allies, men as sponsors – these are the new buzz.

Signs point to a rapid evolution in our concept of leadership. Approaches that move past hierarchy, shift from command and control to collaboration – these leadership behaviors based on "feminine values" (regardless of the gender of the leader displaying them) have been shown to be the most successful in the current era of business (see *The Athena Doctrine* by John Gerzema). We are entering an era of that is beyond categories of gender, mutual understanding via bi-lingual gender communication, and shared vision amongst all who want women to realize the fullest extent of their talents in solving the problems of the world and providing for their families and communities.

Notice that all these trends align with the idea of Go Direct! In this way, you can 'be the change you want to see in the world'.

My challenge to you is: Enjoy to using the tools in this book to show up as her, no matter what is going on around you. Who do you need to be at your Horizon Point in order to have the success and the quality of life you want? Get on the Facebook group for readers (www.facebook.com/groups/confidencecounts/) and enjoy sharing your Horizon Point and success stories. As you now know, you'll get more of the results you desire, with less effort and more connection.

Let's create a movement of empowered women who become leaders, top producers, and community advocates who change the paradigm. Create positive evolution by doing your part to equip current and next generations with tools to make their mark.

Spread the word about this book to friends, family, your daughter/son/niece/nephew/mentee. Gift them a copy. (Note: If you want the shortcuts to apply the concepts in this book to your life AND those of someone you love, we offer a 2 for 1 in our "C-school" (Confidence school) program where you can invite a young, non-employed person to access all the training and coaching calls too. Find out more at **www.sharonmelnick.com/cwc** .)

If you've gotten a lot from the book, leave a review on Amazon about your experience so others can see it will be helpful to them – thank you for doing so!

Keep this book handy as you go through day, you never know when a moment will arise and you want to always be able to have Confidence when it Counts!

Acknowledgements

A huge and heartfelt thank you to those of you who have shared and supported me in my dream to launch a Confidence Revolution for Women worldwide:

Those of you who endorsed these ideas early on and brought me to your organization to train, especially Cornelia Ecker, Heidi Piper, and the women's leadership team at Procter and Gamble; Charlotte Hawthorne of Eli Lilly; Cindy Pace of MetLife; Stacy Francis of Allied Professional Women; Andrea March of the Women's Leadership Exchange; Carolyn Schaefer of York Traditions Bank; Aileen Cabelly of Colgate; YaleWomen organizing committee; and Nancy Hedlund who spearheaded the Confident Leader Assessment at Baxter.

To my game-changers: Laurie Cooke, Liz Stueck, Liz Coyle (and the organizing committee) of the Healthcare Businesswomen's Association, and Janet Wigfield of the National Association of Female Executives and Multicultural Women's Conference for inviting me to keynote their Leadership conferences on "Confidence". To Janet Riccio of Omnicom, the center of 'cool', and a game-changing connector for me.

To my clients whose names and circumstances have been changed for anonymity, but who have shared their challenges and their wins with me. You've enabled me to understand the phenomenon and see the tools in action to transform your lives. I thank you for the trust you placed in me and for allowing me to be a part of the contribution that you've been put here to make. To hundreds of clients and trainees in "C-school" and the Confident Influential Leader program who lived the stories I shared in the book. And my subscribers who provided feedback on the book title – sharing creative ideas, direction, and brimming enthusiasm to keep me going. It's for you that I get up each day.

To Louise for her never ending inspiration to change women's lives around the world and for everyday acts of courage. To Jennifer Hartwell, my most trusted advisor, who generously gave her insight, perspective, and the pulse of professional women. A lifelong thank you to my parents Susan and Neil, for their never-ending support, including during my psychology degree and research at Harvard Medical School that informs this mission of my life.

To my mentor Karlen Lyons-Ruth, PhD who has done more than anyone else to put together the pieces of the intergenerational cycle, and included me in the research that describes what parents bring with them from childhood that interferes with success as adults - this formed the basis for the idea of Confidence Types. And Livingston Grant from Harvard Medical School that enabled me to do the foundational research that led to the development of some of the ideas herein.

To the giants on whose shoulders I stand – Sheryl Sandberg for genuinely sharing her inner soundtrack and creating a firestorm. Joan Williams whose pioneering work reified the phenomena of bias. Katty Kay and Claire Shipman whose book on women and confidence expanded our insights and put the subject on the map. Gloria Feldt who shares the bigger vision and has a brilliant solution for women to change the paradigm. Brene Brown who has brought self-awareness and the prospect of less self-pressure to so many women.

To the passionate research and communication teams at Catalyst, McKinsey, Bain and Company, KPMG, EY, and Working Mother who have revealed insights about the progress and challenges to women's advancement. With a special shout out to Jan Combopiano for her vast knowledge and dedication, and for including me in the Catalyst conferences to stay on the cutting edge of research.

To the editors and writers of the NY Times, Forbes, Financial Times, and Harvard Business Review for covering the topic of all things related to women's advancement so that myself and other citizens can stay informed on a daily basis about the contributions of smart women, the pervasiveness of gender bias, and it's effects. To the Experts who shared their thought leadership for this book: Marcelle Pick, Ob/Gyn NP; Holly Buchanan, Author; Kate Orenstein, Op-Ed project

To my speaker's bureaus who have believed in my message and provided a megaphone for reaching influencers.

To Michele who is a treasure of an assistant and partner in my business. Thank you for putting up with all my last-minute requests and always having my back. And for helping to find and organize some of the key research in the book.

To JJ Virgin, Karl Krummenacher, Kellyann Petrucci and the Mindshare Mastermind for inspiration and the path to creating a book that impacts many people. Big shout out to my book writing buddies who provided support – logistic and emotional - during the kickoff and throughout the book writing process – Nicole Beurkens, Robyn Benson, Ann Shippy, Sheila Kilbane, Debora Wayne, Joan Rosenberg, RitaMarie Loscalzo. To Nalini Chilkov and Shiroko Shokitch for the idea of women "Rising Above". JJ - thank you for role-modelling a limitless mindset and inviting me to share my ideas on your Mindshare stage.

To Mike Koenigs and his team for providing the infrastructure and blueprint to create a bestselling book – and for showing the possibilities a book can open to create a movement.

My extra special appreciation and smiles to Jane for providing the hearth: this book would never have been possible without your belief in the quality of my dream and my ability to carry it out, your generous support, prodding to "focus!", and frequent sacrifice for the cause.

Endnotes

[i] Lyons-Ruth, Karlen, et al. "From Infant Attachment Disorganization to Adult Dissociation: Relational Adaptations or Traumatic Experiences?" *The Psychiatric Clinics of North America* 29.1 (2006): 63; Lyons-Ruth, K, et al. "Childhood Experiences of Trauma and Loss Have Different Relations to Maternal Unresolved and Hostile-Helpless States of Mind on The AAI." *Attachment & Human Development* 5.4 (2003): 330-352

[ii] Melnick, Sharon. *Success Under Stress: Powerful Tools for Staying Calm, Confident, and Productive When the Pressure's On.* Saranac Lake, NY: AMACOM Publishing, 2013.

[iii] Keyes, Corey, Barbara L. Fredrickson, and Nansook Park. "Positive psychology and the quality of life." *Handbook of social indicators and quality of life research.* Springer Netherlands, 2012. 99-112.

[iv] Mohr, Tara. *Playing Big: Practical Wisdom for Women Who Want to Speak Up, Create, and Lead.* Garden City, NY: Avery Publishing, 2015.

[v] Mohr, Tara. "Why Women Don't Apply for Jobs Unless They're 100% Qualified." *Harvard Business Review*, August 25, 2014, https://hbr.org/2014/08/why-women-dont-apply-for-jobs-unless-theyre-100-qualified/

[vi] "What Moms Choose: The Working Mother Report." Mother Research Institute, 2011. http://www.wmmsurveys.com/WhatMomsChoose.pdf

[vii] Dunham, Lena. *Don't Take it Personally When I Tell You "No." I'm Using it On Everyone This Year,* January 20, 2016 https://www.linkedin.com/pulse/say-life-lena-dunham,

[viii] Cummings, Whitney, *Whitney Cummings: Miss Codependence,* Lenny Letter.com http://www.lennyletter.com/health/a182/whitney-cummings-miss-codependence/

43472617R00118

Made in the USA
Middletown, DE
10 May 2017